Samantha Brown
with Libby Koch

Women's Guide
TO GOING IT ALONE

HOW ANY WOMAN CAN PROTECT
HER MONEY AND HER FUTURE

Published by:

[WP] Wilkinson Publishing Pty Ltd
ACN 006 042 173
Level 4, 2 Collins Street
Melbourne, Vic 3000

Tel: 03 9654 5446   www.wilkinsonpublishing.com.au

Copyright © 2008 Samantha Brown and Libby Koch

All rights reserved. No part of this publication may be reproduced, stored in a retrieval system or transmitted in any form by any means without the prior permission of the copyright owner. Enquiries should be made to the publisher.

Every effort has been made to ensure that this book is free from error or omissions. However, the Publisher, the Author, the Editor or their respective employees or agents, shall not accept responsibility for injury, loss or damage occasioned to any person acting or refraining from action as a result of material in this book whether or not such injury, loss or damage is in any way due to any negligent act or omission, breach of duty or default on the part of the Publisher, the Author, the Editor, or their respective employees or agents.

The Author, the Publisher, the Editor and their respective employees or agents do not accept any responsibility for the actions of any person - actions which are related in any way to information contained in this book.

National Library of Australia Cataloguing-in-Publication data:
Author: Brown, Samantha.
Title: Women's guide : to going it alone / Samantha Brown ; Libby Koch.
ISBN: 9781921332302 (pbk.).
Subjects: Divorced women--Finance, Personal--Handbooks, manuals, etc..
                Widows--Finance, Personal--Handbooks, manuals, etc.
                Women--Finance, Personal--Handbooks, manuals, etc.
                Saving and investment--Australia--Handbooks, manuals, etc.
Other Authors/Contributors: Koch, Libby.
Dewey Number: 332.0240082

Cover design: Paul Harvey, page design: Chris Georgiou

CONTENTS

About The Authors v
Alone by David Koch vi

Step 1.   First 24 Hours or So 1
            Separation from your partner
            Death of your partner

Step 2.   Get Organised 9
            Get it together
            Know your rights
            Put together a team
            Learn about the process
            Learn how to budget
            Budget planner
            If you reconcile

Step 3.   What You're Entitled To 53
            Dividing the assets
            Everyday assets
            Bank accounts
            Investments
            Superannuation
            Family business
            Family trusts
            Maintenance

Step 4.	Providing For Your Children	.91
	Reaching an agreement	
	Who is financially responsible for your children?	
	How much you are entitled to per child	
	Government support	
Step 5.	Investing Your Share	.117
	Pay off the house	
	Investing in the stockmarket	
	Investing in property	
	Put it into super	
	Buy a business	
	Estate planning	
Step 6.	Dividing Responsibilities	.145
	Counselling	
	Co-parenting	
	Time with the kids	
	Adult children	
Step 7.	Making Sure it Doesn't Happen Again	.155
	Moving on	
	Entering another relationship	
	Preparing for marriage	
	Bottom Line by Libby Koch	.169
	Tables and Contact List	.171

ABOUT THE AUTHORS

Samantha Brown

Samantha Brown followed her father, well-known financial expert David Koch, into the world of finance journalism at a young age.

Samantha began her career as a personal finance writer, co-authoring the Australian bestseller *The Teenager's Guide to Money*. She followed that up with *The Teenager's Guide to Part Time Jobs*, *Leaving Home: The Ultimate Guide*, and *Travel and Working Holidays: The Ultimate Guide*.

Samantha has spent the past six years working as a television and radio reporter for Sky News and Bloomberg News in Sydney and Hong Kong, covering Asian and Australian stock markets and business news.

Last year Samantha and her husband undertook their biggest challenge, the birth of daughter Matilda.

Libby Koch

Libby Koch is a nurse by training and currently works as David's PA. Just as important, Libby is the master of the Koch family finances and budget. Apart from allocating David his allowance, she masterminded the financial tightrope of balancing a single income while raising four kids (Samantha, Brianna, Alexander and Georgie) and meeting the mortgage. For many years Libby wrote a weekly home budgeting column for News Ltd newspapers.

Libby has also co-authored *Your Money and Your Life*, *I'm not made of Money* and *Kochie's Guide*.

ALONE

By David Koch

In past generations marriage was 'till death do us part'. These days it's often 'till we serve each other divorce papers'. Gee how times have changed.

Almost half of all marriages end up in divorce. That's a pretty amazing statistic. In 2006, 51,375 Australian couples divorced. The same year there were 114,222 marriages. It's not just newlyweds changing their mind. Around 45 percent of couples getting divorced have been married for over 10 years.

My wife Libby and I have beaten the odds and been married 29 years… touch wood. But we've been through a period where many of our good friends haven't been so fortunate. It seems kids leaving school is a critical time of analysis for many couples and they decide their future is to part, despite being married for so long. It seems bringing up children may have masked problems in the relationship.

We've had a stream of female friends come to us at separation in a panic of worry. Often they don't know where their money is and how they can access it. Many are not the primary breadwinner in the relationship and have had little involvement in the family finances.

They are alone and vulnerable. In any divorce negotiations their partner instantly has the upper hand because they have the information. This book tries to even the balance and provide the information you need to be able to negotiate on equal terms.

Unfortunately, if you're reading this book it means you have probably separated from your partner. But, as I'm sure you've gathered, you are not alone.

Most people separate because of poor communication and conflict. Before you go any further, you need to make a conscious effort to do what you can to improve your relationship. As you will see from this book, the divorce process is very complicated and costly. The better your relationship with your ex-partner, the less emotionally and financially draining the journey will be.

This book will help you through the separation and divorce process. It provides information and guidance on each step along the way. It will also bring your financial knowledge up-to-scratch, now you don't have a partner to help make decisions about your financial future.

The book follows the divorce process of five women; Diane, Jane, Karen, Sarah and Rebecca. These are all real life case studies, but the names have been changed for privacy reasons. These women were selected because their divorces and financial situations are very different. Their experiences can help you work out what to do and what not to do.

It also looks at how to take control of your finances if you are alone following the death of your partner. We cover the steps you need to take straight after a death and the financial skills you need to equip yourself with going forward. We will teach you how to do everything from setting up a bank account to budgeting for your household. We will also help you understand your investments and what you should do with them.

STEP 1

FIRST 24 HOURS OR SO

First 24 Hours Or So | **STEP 1**

SEPARATION FROM YOUR PARTNER

Under no circumstances should you spend the first 24 hours after you have separated from your partner locked away in your room. You have to take action.

There are a number of things you have to do straight away. If your partner left you, he may have been planning his departure for a while and could have even received legal advice already.

- ❏ Take money out of your bank account to get you through the first few weeks, but try and be fair. For example, if there is $10,000 in a bank account only take out $5,000.

- ❏ Change the password on your bank accounts. The last thing you want him to do is spend all your savings on himself.

- ❏ Apply to the bank to change your accounts to two signatories. This means that both you and your partner have to sign any cheques or withdrawals from your accounts.

- ❏ Organise with the bank to receive all correspondence relating to all your accounts. This includes credit card bills, cheque and savings account statements, mortgage updates, and superannuation statements.

- ❏ Collect as many papers as possible and make copies of the lot. We're talking about things like the deeds to the family home and any investment properties, share certificates, and super fund details.

- ❏ Secure all of your paperwork. It's advisable to take it away from your family home to your parent's place or to a close friend.

- ❏ Secure things that are important to you like jewellery, photos, and family videos.

- ❏ If your partner's moved out, change the locks. You don't have a legal right to do this, but it will make your home more secure.

Women's Guide To Going it Alone

- ❑ Make an appointment to see an accredited solicitor and psychologist.

- ❑ Don't agree to anything without taking time to think about it and get advice. You never know, he may have already been to a lawyer who has advised him to take advantage of your shock.

- ❑ Be fair if he is moving out of the family home. Let him take some stuff, like the second television and some crockery.

- ❑ Don't say anything really bad about the other person in front of your kids. This is the most emotionally exposed you are ever likely to be…so curb your tongue.

- ❑ Be careful about verbal threats. If you are genuinely scared or intimidated contact the AVO officer at your local police station.

- ❑ Keep the lines of communication open. If you do this you will increase the chance of an amicable separation. You don't want to pass a message on to your partner through your solicitor, who speaks to his solicitor, who relays the message to your partner. That drastically increases the chance of miscommunication, which can lead to litigation. It's also really expensive!

- ❑ If your break-up is civilised and you have children, take them to see where their dad is living. Reassure them that he is not sleeping on the streets. Little kids need to see he has a fridge, a television and a bed.

- ❑ Let their school know what is happening. The school should then ask teachers and the school counsellor to offer your kids extra support. Teachers also need to be kept in the loop so they can monitor any changes in children's behaviour or schoolwork.

First 24 Hours Or So | **STEP 1**

Family business

Are you a director of the family business? Do you hold shares in it? Do you hold a position of responsibility? If you answered yes to any of those questions, there are a number of things you have to do in the first 24 hours or so to protect your interest in the business.

Remember, while you need to protect your interest, you don't want to cripple the business.

- ❑ Change all business bank accounts to two signatories. This means you have to sign all cheques and authorise all withdrawals.

- ❑ Organise for the bank to copy you in on any correspondence.

- ❑ Do not raid the business bank account. You can't take money out in case it hurts the running of the business.

- ❑ Limit liabilities or access to debt, especially if your business is secured against the family home. Limit the business overdraft at the bank.

- ❑ Get your hands on any documentation of business assets and make copies.

- ❑ Do not go to court and freeze the business from operating. That can spell the end of the business.

- ❑ If the business is some kind of importer, get a court order to stop your partner transferring money out of the country.

Women's Guide To Going it Alone

Death of your partner

The loss of a partner is similar to a divorce in many ways. You need to sort out your financial affairs, deal with lawyers, split the assets according to the will, take control of your finances and plan for the future.

Financially, you are likely to be much better off than in a divorce situation. Generally, all assets will go to the surviving spouse or partner and not have to be split up. Things like your place of residence, your partner's superannuation, and your investments. You are also likely to receive a life insurance payout.

Find the will

As soon as you can you need to locate your husband's will. If his will has not been updated since your marriage, don't worry your marriage overrides it.

If you find that your husband has not left any kind of will, you must apply to the Probate Division of the Supreme Court to be made executor of the estate. The Court will then issue you letters of administration and appointment.

Any real estate you jointly owned will automatically go to you, the surviving spouse. This includes the family home and any investment properties.

When it comes to wills, de facto partners are given similar rights to spouses. If a will can't be located, de facto relationships are recognised as family relationships and de facto partners can inherit property in certain situations.

Locate Life Insurance Policy

You don't have to be rich and famous just to have a life insurance policy. Most people have at least a small policy tied to their super fund.

If your partner was only insured through his super policy, the payout will probably be one or two times his annual salary. If he had a specific life insurance policy, that payout will be much larger.

This money, in effect, has to make up for not being able to receive any kind of maintenance going forward…like you would receive in a divorce situation.

Locate your husband's life insurance policy and notify the insurer of his death. The insurer will then process the claim and pay a lump-sum to the beneficiary (most likely you). This money is tax-free and can be used for any propose. For example your can use it to pay off debt like your mortgage or to cover your everyday living costs.

Once you have located the will and the life insurance policy, contact the accountant who handles your partner's affairs and seek advice.

STEP 2

GET ORGANISED

STEP 2 — Get Organised

GET IT TOGETHER

You and your partner have made the decision to separate. If the move was unexpected you've completed the first 24 hours checklist. Now you have to work on getting your life together.

Who lives where?

As soon as you and your partner make the decision to separate, work out who is going to live where temporarily. Unfortunately most of us don't have multiple houses, like Tom Cruise and Nicole Kidman, so it's not a case of who's going to live in the city residence and who's going to move into the beach house.

If there are children involved, decide who's going to be looking after them full-time. It is often best for this parent to stay in the family home with the kids, so their lives are disrupted as little as possible.

This means the other partner needs to move into some other temporary accommodation. You need to ensure this temporary accommodation isn't too extravagant, so it's not a drain on your combined finances.

If you and your partner proceed with a divorce, be prepared for the living situation to change once the property settlement occurs later down the track, as you may decide to sell your family home.

Short-term finances

When you have worked out who is going to live where, you need to sit down and talk about who is going to pay for what over the coming months. This is particularly important if one partner is in paid work and the other is not.

Discuss things like how you are going to make debt commitments on things like your home, cars and credit cards. How are you going to pay for the upkeep of your children and yourselves?

If children are involved, you and your partner will need to reach an initial agreement on child support. That is the amount of money the full-time carer will receive from the other parent to help cover the cost of feeding, clothing, educating and housing the kids.

The government's Child Support Agency (CSA) has a really helpful website (www.csa.gov.au). It has a calculator function you can use to get an estimate of how much child support should be paid.

If you and your partner can't agree on an appropriate figure for child support together, you need to make an official application with the Child Support Agency. You can do this online. The CSA will then do an assessment of how much money you should receive, depending on things like your partner's income and how many children you have.

> **If you're lucky, and it's an amicable separation, you may be able keep your current financial structure ...**

If you and your partner do not have any children, but you can't afford to look after yourself, you can apply for spousal maintenance. It takes two to three weeks to get to court for an interim order for spousal maintenance.

If your partner stops paying the mortgage, and tells the court he has no money, the court may be able to stop the bank from selling your home. For example, if your house is worth $500,000 and your mortgage is just $50,000, you can apply to the court for an injunction to stop the house being sold, because the bank is not really at risk.

If you're lucky, and it's an amicable separation, you may be able keep your current financial structure until the property settlement. Just dip into your savings to cover the cost of temporary accommodation for the other partner, and both use your everyday bank accounts like normal.

> Karen thought she and her husband were happily married. That's until it became all too obvious he was having an affair at work. Karen forgave him and got on with her life. They had another baby to go with their family of two daughters. Then Karen found out her husband was having another affair.
>
> Karen had thought she was partnered for life. She now realised they needed to stay apart and made the agonising decision to separate.
>
> Karen was a trained nurse, but became a full-time mum after having kids. She had always looked after the bills and luckily money wasn't an issue at the time of separating. She just kept on doing the bills and the family's banking, having access to spending money as per normal.
>
> Even after getting their divorce, Karen and her ex-husband didn't rush into a financial settlement. He wished to cause her as little trouble as possible. He paid all the family's expenses and Karen had access to his credit card account for her needs as well as family necessities. It's all about trust says Karen, and it works both ways. "We discuss how our money is going and it has always been thought of as OUR money. The important thing is to keep the channels for discussion open".

The reality is most separations aren't as amicable as Karen's. If you and your partner are arguing over money, get a pen and paper and specifically write down who is allowed to take what out of the combined finances. Make sure both signatures are required on all withdrawals from the account.

Women's Guide To Going it Alone

Tell the kids

Don't leave your children out of the loop. No matter how painful it is, tell them about your decision to separate as soon as you have worked out the immediate details of your family's new living situation.

Long before you and your partner officially separate, your children are likely to have some idea of what's going on. They absorb the arguments and the tension around them. Many children sense something terrible is happening.

When you tell your children about the decision to separate, do it together. Choose a familiar setting, which doesn't have any distractions.

Start by talking about events the kids have probably noticed, like fighting or sleeping in separate rooms. This will help the children connect to what they are being told.

Relationships Australia offers advice on how to manage separation (www.relationships.com.au). They say you should try and convey the reason you are separating in a simple way. Leave out the bits that blame the other parent. Make statements such as "we like each other in some ways, but can't live together". Say some of the things that happened between you are hard to explain and you know it won't be easy for them to understand.

They need time to actually hear the news ...

Children react differently to situations of change at different stages of their life and development. They may take some time to process information about the collapse of their parents' marriage. They need time to actually hear the news, absorb it, ask questions, and then begin to comprehend what the event will mean.

Encourage them to ask questions, but don't be alarmed if most of their initial questions are about the practical side of your decision. Things like where they will be living, who they will see on Christmas, what happens to the annual family holiday. This doesn't mean they don't care about why you're separating, but rather they are trying to secure themselves.

Assure your children again and again that you and your partner will always love them and the bond between a parent and a child can't be broken. Tell them separation or divorce is an adult issue. Make them understand that they are not responsible.

> **She now realised they needed to stay apart and made the agonising decision to separate.**

Make sure you ask your kids what you and your partner can do to help them during this difficult time in their lives.

When Karen and her husband made the decision to separate they sat their three young daughters down and explained to them that dad had to live elsewhere.

Karen says, "our eldest daughter was very angry but the others were too little to understand what was really happening. She was amazing when she saw how I wasn't coping and filled in for me when I could hardly get out of bed in the mornings. She got the others up and dressed and started breakfast for them, and her being all of eight years old! The day I felt back on track she almost immediately went back to being a little girl".

Karen believes the key to happiness for all of them, particularly the children, is to try and see the good side of the other partner and not write them off completely. The more you talk about your partner's faults, especially in front of the children, the more bitterness grows.

Tell everyone else

The next step is to explain the situation to your friends and family.

Try to encourage your nearest and dearest not to take sides. A couple we know separated and several family members and friends took sides. They ended up getting back together and had a strained relationship with those who supported one partner over the other.

When you tell everyone else, try to develop a support network. It is important to talk to people and feel supported. That will help you work through the grieving and adjustment process.

If you have the kids full-time, you will have to get used to being a single parent. Take up offers of support from your friends and family, whether it's offers to babysit or to pick the kids up from school.

Counselling

You and your children do not have to go through the separation process on your own; go and get professional help for everyone involved.

When it comes to your kids, a good place to start is with the school counsellor. They are there to offer support and advice on anything that affects their pupils. In the end, at home issues often end up affecting schoolwork.

> **It is important to talk to people and feel supported.**

Book in a time to chat with the school counsellor without your children. Explain the situation and try and provide details on how you think the news of the separation is affecting them. The counsellor should then organise to meet with your kids on a regular basis.

It's important not to forget to look after yourself. This is especially important if you have children; you need to be able to be there when they need you.

Go and see someone who can help you deal with the issues associated with the separation process. Things like regaining control of your life, dealing with feelings of anger towards your ex-partner, a sense of abandonment, and aloneness.

Speak to friends, or friends of friends, who have been through the separation process. Find out what counsellors they used and whether they were any good. You can also contact your local community centre or the local doctor for details of appropriate counsellors. Relationships Australia has branches around the country. It receives funding from the government to help it provide services such as family relationships counselling.

You could also try help groups. The support of a group of people, who are going through the same issues, can give you a big boost. You'll find out, unfortunately, you're not alone.

Marriage counselling

Separation does not always mean divorce. Speak to your partner about seeing a marriage counsellor. You never know, you may be able to save your relationship if you put in the work.

A marriage counsellor can act as a mediator and help you work through issues that you and your partner have trouble discussing calmly or are unable to resolve. Relationships Australia also has mediators that can help resolve family disputes.

If you and your partner decide to reconcile, a marriage counsellor can give you tips on how to resolve an argument calmly and what you should do when you can't agree. It's a good idea to continue seeing the counsellor regularly when you are back together.

Women's Guide To Going it Alone

Jane and her husband had been married for twenty odd years before they finally decided to separate. Their relationship had been in a downward spiral for quite some time. They had irreconcilable differences that lead to many arguments and periods of long silences.

Jane and her husband had nearly ended their marriage several times over the years, but counselling had got them through and they remained together while their children grew to young adults.

The family situation became explosive when their two strong willed teenagers entered the mix with their own agendas. Jane says her husband isolated himself from the family, coping as he saw fit with the situation. In reality, his absences signalled his withdrawal from the group... which eventually became complete.

They tried family and couple counselling, but this time it was without much success. Finally they decided he should move out to let things settle for a while. It never did.

Initially the household breathed a sigh of relief when he left as the arguments ceased. Even the children, who were upset at the split, did enjoy new-found peace at home. After a year of separation, they sold their house to create a financial settlement, much to everyone's distress. Jane had wanted her husband to come home and try again to be a family, but he refused to go back.

Get Organised | **STEP 2**

Get a job

The busier you keep yourself the less time you have to sit around at home thinking about how lonely you are. If you don't already have a job, why not go out and get one?

A job, whether it's part-time or full-time, will help take your mind off your separation. The money that you earn will also give you greater independence and ease any financial stress if you end up getting divorced.

If you're currently a stay-at-home mum, it could be good to start off with a part-time job that will give you a bit of extra cash and hopefully fit in with school and day-care hours. It will also give you some good experience if you need to get a full-time job should your divorce proceed.

Decide what type of employment you want, then look for a job to apply for. The three most important things when you are trying to get a job are your resume, your presentation and the interview.

The aim of a resume is to outline your previous merits and responsibilities, to show a potential employer you're a good person for the job. Sit down at the computer and think about all the relevant experience, qualifications, achievements and life skills you have that would make you a suitable candidate for a particular job.

When you tee up an interview for a job, do not underestimate the importance of presentation. In the eyes of the interviewer, the way you present yourself in an interview situation reflects how you work. This is why it is important to be on time, appropriately dressed, and neat and tidy.

The interview is vital because it gives the employer a chance to see if you are the best person for the job. An employer will ask you questions they think are important. Your responses will help them decide if you are the right person for the job.

Women's Guide To Going it Alone

To prepare yourself for the interview, identify your qualifications, skills and any positive qualities that would set you apart from other people applying for the job. Then do your homework and find out as much as possible about the employer. Look at their website, do an Internet search, and ask your family and friends if they have any information about the company. Then, during the interview, drop little hints that show you've done your homework.

If you have trouble finding a job because you don't have the appropriate qualifications, try doing some volunteer work in an area you're interested in. Many people take on voluntary positions to build up experience to help them get a paid job. It will also give you stimulation.

Karen and her husband had an amicable divorce. Her husband generously supported the family financially, but he still had to pay for two households. Karen decided she needed to return to the workforce to add to their income and to earn extra money for things like holidays.

Karen was a nurse by training and decided to go back to her old profession. She decided part-time work, when her daughters were at school, was the best option. Karen found there was a high demand for home nurses and she wouldn't have to update her skills for the job. She got a position three days a week working from 8am to 2pm assisting elderly patients. That allowed her to drop her girls at school on her way to work and always be there when they finished.

KNOW YOUR RIGHTS

Under no circumstances should you allow yourself to be bullied by your partner at any time during your separation or divorce proceedings. He cannot cut-off your access to money or take your children away. You have specific financial and custodial rights.

Financial rights

Maintenance

As soon as you and your partner separate you can apply for spousal and child maintenance.

Spousal maintenance is where your partner helps support you financially because you don't have the skills or work experience to support yourself.

You receive child support from your partner if you are the full-time carer of your kids. This money is meant to help cover the cost of feeding, clothing, educating and housing your children.

Access to Documents

There are a number of documents, or at least copies of documents, that you can demand access to. At least two days before your first Court date you must both have the following documents:

- ☐ Your three most recent tax returns and assessments
- ☐ Superannuation documents
- ☐ Financial statements for any businesses, trusts or partnerships
- ☐ Any Business Activity Statements for the 12-months ending immediately before the first court date

- ☐ For any corporation, its most recent annual return, listing directors and shareholders, and corporation's memorandum and articles of association

- ☐ For any trust, the trust deed

- ☐ For any partnership, the partnership agreement

- ☐ A market appraisal for any item of property in which either you or your partner have an interest

Property Settlement

The property settlement doesn't just cover real estate, it's all your assets. Everything from the family home to shares and your superannuation.

> **List all your big assets and how much they are worth.**

There is no formula used to divide your assets and work out how much of the property settlement you are entitled to. You and your partner can sit down and try to work out how your property should be divided.

If you can't come to an agreement, you can get help from solicitors or turn to the courts. They will listen to all the evidence and then make fair decisions based on the unique facts of your case.

Disputes in the Family Court look at what you've got and what you owe, direct financial contributions to the marriage, indirect financial contributions to the marriage like inheritance, and non-financial contributions to the marriage such as looking after your kids. The court will also consider your family's future requirements like your age, ability to earn an income and care of the children.

A leading financial planner we spoke with said he has never seen a property settlement that can't be reduced to a sheet of paper. List all your big assets and how much they are worth. Next to each asset write whether you or your partner will take it, or whether it will be split 50/50. Then total each person's share to make sure you roughly get the same amount.

If you try to do a deal yourselves, you will keep channels of communication open and save heaps in legal fees. You don't want to turn an asset pool of $500,000 into a $50,000 legal matter.

Custody rights

It is best for everyone if you and your partner can work out a permanent arrangement for your children at the start. You should avoid having one set-up during your separation period, and then changing that when you make a permanent custody arrangement later on.

Who gets the kids?

There are no set rules about who should get the kids. The only given is the Court will always make decisions based on what is in the best interests of the child.

The Court also considers the wishes of your children, and where they want to live. The amount of weight given will depend on whether your kids are old enough to make this decision maturely.

Custody can be split 50/50 or any way you and your partner, or the Court, feel is in the best interest of your kids. Bear in mind the Court is generally reluctant to remove children from a situation where they are happy and settled, or split up siblings.

Access by the other parent

The Court considers contact with family members to be the right of a child, not the right of a parent. The Court usually finds it is in a child's best interest to maintain contact with both parents.

Generally, contact will only be denied in extreme cases. For example, an abusive parent may not be allowed contact with their children.

PUT TOGETHER A TEAM

Once you've told everyone about your plans to separate and have your short-term finances in order, the next step is to put together your support team.

We are not talking about babysitters and counsellors this time, but your lawyer, accountant and financial planner. The saying goes 'don't get mad, get even'… you will need these guys to help you do that.

If you have been widowed, you will also need the help of these professionals to get your life back on track. A lawyer will facilitate the distribution of assets, an accountant will help you manage your tax situation, and a financial planner will help you plan for your financial future.

Do your research

Don't just hire the accountant or lawyer up at your local shops; you have to do your research and find the best person to handle your situation.

Start by asking your friends and family who they use and if they are happy with the service. Better yet, quiz any divorced friends about their team.

If you know or are related to a lawyer, accountant or financial planner, don't feel like you have to use them. In many cases it's often best not to. Although they may give you a good discount on their services, or even offer them for free, they may not have the right qualifications and experience to help you.

The Internet is a great research tool. Most professional or industry bodies have a website that allows you to search for particular professionals in your area. When putting your team together try and find people who specialise in divorce.

> A friend recommended a lawyer for Karen to see, which was a disaster. It didn't take long for her to see it was in the lawyer's interest to keep dragging out the process of divorcing her husband. The lawyer would often say "you deserve this and should stand your ground, I'll write to your husband with our demands".
>
> Karen says this was like a red rag to a bull, and caused problems between her and her husband that hadn't been there. She knew the situation wasn't right and, after dismissing this lawyer, found a more gentle female solicitor who handled her legal matters without pushing other agendas.

Lawyer

You don't have to have a lawyer to guide your through the divorce process. If you are familiar with the process, you can represent yourself in your family law case. There are also courses you can do through legal aid centres that teach you how to represent yourself in court.

If you have no legal background and are struggling to cope with your separation and the associated changes, it's a good idea to get a lawyer. They can manage your divorce proceedings and your legal correspondence.

When looking for a lawyer make sure you find one who specialises in dealing with family law matters. Start by asking friends or relatives if they know of anyone. The Law Council of Australia or the law society in your state may be able to recommend someone. The website of the Family Law Section of the Law Council of Australia allows you to search for family lawyers in your area and gives you their contact details (www.familylawsection.org.au).

The number one thing to look for in a lawyer is dispute resolution skills. This may keep you from going through the emotional and financial upheaval of going to court.

Women's Guide — To Going it Alone

If you can't afford a lawyer, there are other options available. Community Legal Centres offer free advice. They may be able to help with things like preparing documents, negotiating on your behalf and representing you in court. Many centres provide direct legal assistance over the phone or can suggest other services that can help. Phone the nearest centre for information about their services. Look them up in the whitepages under Legal Centres (Community).

You can also get free legal advice from Legal Aid. Simply contact your nearest Legal Aid office and make an appointment. Advice is generally limited to around 20 minutes. If you need more than basic information, officially apply for legal aid by completing a legal aid application form. This assesses things like your financial means and whether your case is likely to succeed (and their costs can be justified). If you are granted legal aid, you will then have access to a lawyer who will help you with the case. You may have to contribute to the cost of their time.

The services offered by Legal Aid may differ from state to state. For example, in Victoria some of the legal aid offices present free divorce classes aimed at people who wish to make their own application for divorce.

Accountant

You need an accountant to come in and look at your financial situation, value your assets and liabilities, and give you advice on tax issues.

An accountant will also help you determine just how much money you require from your partner to support yourself. It's amazing how many people don't have a clue what it costs them to live, they just spend as they need and always seem to get by. You need to work out exactly how much money you need to live on each year, so you know what to ask for when it comes time do the financial settlement.

An accountant will also give you advice on the most tax effective way to structure the financial settlement. When you are dividing up your assets make sure you know how much you bought each item for, it's current market value, and whether you will have to pay tax on the gain when you go to sell it at a later date. You need to be careful you don't get an asset with a large unrealised gain in it, while your partner gets the asset with no unrealised gain, as you will end up with a big tax bill when you go to sell and he won't. If you do end up taking an asset with an unrealised gain, that has to be taken into account in the financial settlement and you have to be compensated accordingly.

Jenny Wheatley is a forensic accountant at WHK Horwath Corporate Finance. She says there are certain hoops you need to jump through to get a good tax result. For people who are financially inexperienced there are lots of tricks and traps around, so make sure you get proper advice.

Just like there are different types of doctors, there are different types of accountants. There are accountants who work for your local butcher and there are ones who look after investment banks. You need to make sure your accountant has experience dealing with your situation and they have either a CPA or a CA qualification.

> An accountant will also give you advice on the most tax effective way to structure the financial settlement.

You can search for an accountant on the CPA website, www.cpaaustralia.com.au.

Don't use the family accountant you and your partner used. You need someone who is independent and 100 percent on your side. It is also against the Institute of Chartered Accountants Code of Ethics for an accountant to advise two clients who are in a dispute.

Financial Planner

A financial planner looks at your financial situation and develops a plan to grow your savings to meet your goals. They invest your money on your behalf, and monitor gains and losses.

A family lawyer can fight for what you want, but you need a financial planner to help you work out what's worth fighting for. They will help you work out how much money you need to live off each year, and the lump sum you need to ask for in the property settlement. A financial planner can also help you work out whether you should do things like split your superannuation, sell your home or get out of the family business.

The Financial Planning Association website is a really good place to start searching for a planner. If you go to www.fpa.asn.au you can do a search to find financial planning companies close to you, who provide the type of advice you need. The Australian Securities and Investments Commission (ASIC) must license all people giving financial advice.

Remember it's your money, so take an interest. There are lots of people out there dying to help you manage your money, and you have to decide on the right person. The last think you want is to lose any money.

Shop around and speak to many financial advisors to develop an understanding of how they work, and how they would work for you. It's a positive sign if they can tell you 'what they can do personally' rather than 'how good they are at their job'.

What to look for

When you have narrowed down your search to a couple of lawyers, accountants and financial planners, find out from either their website or over the phone:

- ❏ How much do they charge?
  - How much is it for a consultation
  - How much is it for each hour they spend on your account
  - Do they charge administration fees
- ❏ What experience have they had in divorce or separation cases?

- ❏ Do they have references or testimonials from past clients that you can read?
- ❏ What accreditation do they have?
- ❏ How long have they been in business?
- ❏ Down the track, are there any barriers to taking your business elsewhere?

The initial meeting

Once you have decided on a lawyer, accountant and financial planner you will have an initial meeting with each. This will give you a chance to check you have made the right decision. Make sure you take copies of all relevant documents to this meeting.

They will probably ask you if you would like to sign on with them as a client then and there, but don't feel like you have to commit to them on the spot. You can always say you would like some time to think about your decision.

In this meeting confirm all the details like pricing and whether there are any barriers to taking your business elsewhere later on. Talk about your different options. When you see your lawyer, ask what happens next and how long it's likely to take to deal with your legal matter.

Take notes of everything that is said to you, so you can refer back to them later on. If you don't understand something that is said, ask for clarification. Remember the only stupid question is the one that goes unasked.

Once you have signed up your team, they should get to work on your situation straight away.

LEARN ABOUT THE PROCESS

Technically a marriage can be dissolved by divorce or by nullity, which is where the court finds there was no legal marriage to start with. Today most dissolutions are by divorce.

The Family Law Act 1975 established the principle of no-fault divorce. This means the court does not consider which partner was at fault and why the marriage broke down.

Couples who have been married for less than two years have to see a counsellor to discuss the chances of reconciliation before they can get a divorce. If they don't speak to a counsellor, they have to get special permission from the Family Law Courts to apply for a divorce.

> **You and your partner can still live together under one roof during the separation period**

The only grounds for divorce is the irretrievable breakdown of the relationship, which means there is no reasonable likelihood of the couple getting back together. To prove this, you have to be separated for 12 months. This doesn't have to be a continuous period.

You and your partner can still live together under one roof during the separation period, but you must be able to show that at least one of you has left the marriage relationship and is living independently. The court will require your friends, neighbours or relatives to verify that you and your partner don't share any of the activities of marriage. Things like sleeping together, shopping, cooking, and eating together. Your case may be strengthened if you can explain why you and your partner stayed under the same roof, such as lack of money to get separate accommodation or to be around to look after the kids.

The courts

The Family Court was established in 1975 and is the highest court in Australia that deals with family law issues. The Family Court deals with divorce, children's arrangements after separation and divorce, property settlements after marriage, and spousal maintenance.

One judge hears proceedings. Appeals are heard by the Full Court of the Family Court, which contains three judges.

The Family Court has offices around Australia, known as registries. Western Australia is an exception, as it has its own Family Court. It was created in accordance with the Family Law Act and exercises the same federal jurisdiction as the Family Court of Australia.

Since 2000, the Federal Magistrates Court also deals with family law matters. It aims to provide a quicker and cheaper service, and ease the workload of the Family and Federal Courts.

Most applications under the Family Law Act can be filed in either court. However, only the Family Court deals with disputes concerning property worth more than $700,000 and applications concerning nullity or validity of marriage.

How to keep down costs

You have to pay a fee when you and your partner apply for a divorce. At the moment it's $405 to file an Application for Divorce in the Federal Magistrates Court. You can get out of paying this fee if you are having financial problems or if you hold certain government concession cards.

Don't be fooled, once you add in fees for lawyers and court costs the real price of a divorce is usually much, much more than $405. Divorces can cost as much as $100,000 if you have protracted negotiations or need a court hearing to divide your assets.

Don't panic, there are ways you can keep costs down.

You and your partner can try to work out a financial settlement and custody arrangement for any children by yourselves. Then enlist the help of solicitors to draw up and formalise your agreement.

There are things you can do to reduce your legal costs. For example, you could draft your own documents, do some of your own court appearances, organise market appraisals, carry out investigative work, and do your own photocopying. Some people choose to use a lawyer selectively, only when they really need help. For example, help with application forms or representation at court dates.

You and your partner are able to apply for divorce without the help of lawyers. The Family Court has a free divorce kit to help you through the steps. Contact the court for a copy or go to www.familylawcourts.gov.au . Most community legal centres offer appointments for a free consultation with a lawyer to help you fill out forms or give basic legal advice.

Mediation

Mediation is where a third party helps you and your partner come to an agreement, out of court, about unresolved matters after a separation. The process encourages you to make your own decisions, with the help of professional guidance.

The Family Court provides a number of mediation services. Mediation for issues relating to your children is conducted by a court mediator who is a trained psychologist or social worker. For financial matters, a deputy registrar (court lawyer) may conduct the session.

It's important to note that court mediators are not able to provide legal advice. So you will need to seek your own legal advice during the process.

You will be much better off if you and your partner can successfully reach an agreement though mediation. It greatly reduces the financial and emotional costs of a legal battle.

How to apply for a divorce

1. Complete your application for a divorce. The Family Law Courts' Divorce Kit includes the application form and explains what to do. If you are using a lawyer they should look after this for you.

2. Sign the forms in front of a lawyer or a justice of the peace.

3. Return the forms, in person or by post, to a family law registry with two photocopies and your marriage certificate.

4. Pay the application fee. This is $405 for an Application For Divorce in the Federal Magistrates Court. The fee can be waived if it will cause you financial hardship or if you are on a really low income or a pension.

5. The court will give you a file number and a hearing date. The hearing is usually set about 6 to 8 weeks after the application is filed.

6. If you and your partner applied for a divorce together, the court keeps your original application and gives you both a sealed copy. If you apply on your own, you will receive two sealed copies and have to give one to your partner at least 28 days before the hearing date. You and your partner will also receive a pamphlet covering the effects of divorce.

7. You and your partner only have to attend the hearing if one of you made a sole application or you have a child under 18. If you don't have any kids under 18, or if you have made a joint application, you don't have to attend the hearing.

8. If your divorce application is successful, you will be granted a divorce order at your hearing. This order is final one month and one day after it's made.

   Applicants are not always granted a divorce order at their first hearing. The Court may request further information.

For more information on this process or to obtain a Divorce Kit go to the Family Law Courts website at www.familylawcourts.gov.au or call 1300 352 000

Striking an agreement

You and your partner need to reach agreements on how to split your finances and look after your children. The courts will help you resolve any disputes through mediation. If you can't reach an agreement through mediation, you may have to go to trial. This should be a last resort, because it's usually very expensive and emotional.

If you and your partner have started proceedings in the Family Court, you may be advised to attend an information session. This is a short general introduction to the process. It provides information on how the Family Court mediation services may help to resolve disputes, issues concerning the division of property under the Family Law Act, how the Family Court operates, the role of lawyers and how to best use the Court's services.

Case Assessment Conference

The Case Assessment Conference is the first big event for most people who have a case in the Family Court. In your Case Assessment Conference, you and your partner have the opportunity to settle your dispute with the help of a registrar (in property cases) and/or family consultant (in parenting cases). If you and your partner have chosen to have lawyers, they will also take part in the conference

If an agreement is not reached at the conference, further dispute resolution sessions may be proposed. If progress looks unlikely, your case may advance to a decision by a judge at a trial.

Procedural Hearing

If it looks as if an agreement can be reached, a Procedural Hearing is held the same day as your Case Assessment Conference. It is conducted by a registrar, and a family consultant is usually involved if there are children's issues. At the hearing, any agreement reached during the Case Assessment Conference may be made into legally binding orders of the Court and/or orders are made setting out the next step and what must be done to prepare for this.

At the end of the day of negotiations you may leave with an interim or final agreement to your dispute.

Last chance for mediation

If you still haven't reached an agreement, you should have another go at mediation. This is your last stop before a trial. You want to work really hard to resolve your dispute yourselves, instead of going through the emotional stress and financial expense of a trial.

If you are trying to resolve issues relating to your children, you will probably attend child dispute conferences and meetings with a family consultant, who will help you communicate.

If you are only disputing financial issues, you may be sent to financial mediation with a registrar.

You may have to attend a Conciliation Conference if you are trying to agree on issues relating to your children and your finances. Both a registrar and a family consultant will attend.

If this process is taking a while, and it looks like you may be heading to trial, you can apply for interim orders. An interim hearing will be held and the court will make temporary orders while you wait for the final ruling. This can cover issues like where children live, time they spend with both parents, and urgent property matters.

Sent to trial

If you weren't able to reach an agreement, and further mediation looks unlikely to resolve your dispute, a trial notice is then issued. This sets out orders to be dealt with before the pre-trial conference. For example, setting dates for the filing of things such as financial statements and affidavits of witnesses.

The pre-trial conference determines whether the case is ready for trial. If it is ready, a trial date is set usually four to eight weeks later.

A trial then takes place before a judge in the formal setting of a courtroom.

Going to trial

Children

In order for a divorce to be granted, you and your partner must have made suitable arrangements for the future care of your children (under 18) and any other children who lived as part of your family before you separated.

You will have to be able to answer the following:

- ❑ Where and who they live with, whether the home is rented, what facilities it has etc.
- ❑ Arrangements for their supervision
- ❑ How often they see the parent they are not living with
- ❑ How the family is financially supported
- ❑ The amount of maintenance being paid
- ❑ Their progress at school
- ❑ Their general health

If the court is not satisfied that proper arrangements have been made, it can adjourn the hearing until you can come back with more information. You may have to attend counselling.

The court could also grant a decree nisi (a provisional decree giving you a divorce) but delay finalising the divorce until something is done for your children's care.

Get Organised | STEP 2

Finances

The Family Court says you and your partner must exchange copies of the following documents at least 2 days prior to the first court date:

- ❑ Your three most recent taxation returns and assessments

- ❑ Superannuation documents, including the completed Superannuation Information Kit.

- ❑ If you have a business, trust or partnership, financial statements for the last three financial years and any Business Activity Statements for the 12 months ending before the first court date

- ❑ If you have a corporation, its most recent annual return, listing directors and shareholders, and the corporation's constitution

- ❑ For any trust, the trust deed

- ❑ For any partnership, the partnership agreement

- ❑ A market appraisal of any item of property in which a party has an interest.

A divorce will be granted if:

- ❑ Appropriate arrangements have been made for the welfare of any children

- ❑ Either you or your partner is an Australian resident or citizen

- ❑ The documents were served properly

- ❑ There is a marriage certificate

- ❑ The 12 month separation period has been satisfied

Women's Guide — To Going it Alone

Court appearances

Court appearances can be quite daunting if you have never been inside a courtroom before. The most important thing to remember is etiquette. Good etiquette isn't necessarily going to win over the judge, but bad etiquette will certainly put them offside.

Always address a federal magistrate as "Your Honour". When addressing a registrar, refer to them as "Registrar". Another good tip is always to bow your head slightly at the judge when you are leaving or entering the courtroom.

> Jane and her husband were struggling to agree on just about everything, so she looked for a solicitor to help bring about her financial settlement. A family contact suggested someone, and Jane was able to work well with him. Despite the rapport between them, Jane says "it was a bad way to go and I wouldn't recommend it to anybody. If you can nut out a settlement at the beginning, even if you don't think it's as fair as it should be, it is the best solution. The cost of trying to get what you want is huge, and there are no guarantees of getting what you want in the end. The cost is huge financially, emotionally and physically!".
>
> Jane describes going to court as exhausting. She says her costs were in the thousands for her solicitor, the barrister, and court costs. She also had to take time off work to attend each court visit, which added to the financial burden, and take time to prepare affidavits (a written statement of evidence).
>
> Jane and her husband attended court eight times, as an agreement could never be reached between the two of them on how much they should receive in the financial settlement. They had to

resolve issues such as whether dependant adult children should be paid support and who pays for school fees and books for their child under 18. Her husband's superannuation was also a sticking point. Should it be split and all kept as super or should half be paid out as a lump sum to Jane as part of her settlement?

While feeling she'd have been better off without legal representation, Jane says you get to a point where you can't back out. She says her husband would have used that to his advantage, thinking she was ready to give in to the lesser amount he wanted her to settle on. Jane worked out her total costs for that representation were $100,000. Still, Jane does believe it was helpful having a solicitor for the "biggest problem" of working out his payments towards the children's costs. As she would have two dependant adult students at home for up to five years, she pushed the point of her husband's contribution for their up-keep. The court does not get involved in issues relating to adult children.

Jane's financial situation was very lean, so she sought help from Centrelink. She says they were helpful, although the process of applying for anything is a bit confusing and very lengthy. A Family Tax Benefit was organised, and is paid straight into her bank account because she's a single, working mother. She has also been given a Health Care Card that entitles her to extra benefits such as cheaper pharmaceuticals and lower fees for some doctors that don't bulk bill.

Working out how to split their possessions was also difficult. Jane says you start off trying to be rational, but the longer it goes on you fall into the trap of being vindictive. She says it's a very emotional exercise when things have deteriorated between partners. Again a solicitor was helpful here. He wrote up what possessions would go to Jane in the settlement, and this was conditional on her getting what she wanted in other areas.

LEARN HOW TO BUDGET

Importance of budgeting

A budget is a table or chart that attempts to balance your income and your expenses. It lets you see, in black and white, where your money comes from and where it's going. It basically gives you a snapshot of your finances.

If your partner was responsible for looking after your finances, it's even more important for you to put together a budget yourself. This will help you really see what shape you're in financially. It will also show you how much you spend on particular expenses, and will help you determine how much money you need from your partner to help cover these.

Knowing where your money goes helps you to use it in better ways. You'll be stunned at how much money you spend on some things!

A budget can show you exactly where you can change spending habits. After you've done a budget, you will fall into one of three main categories (we all fit these):

- ❏ You're lucky, and your income is greater than your total expenses. You have money left over at the end of each month after buying all your essential expenses and a few little luxuries. Set a couple of goals on what to do with this spare cash, for example saving up for a big holiday or putting extra money into your super.

- ❏ Thinks don't look so good. Your expenses are more than your income, but you are covering essentials. In this situation you need to look at all those little luxuries you're buying and see if you can cut down. Keep the essentials, prune the luxuries and you'll have a bit left over to save or put towards the credit card bill you never seem able to pay off.

Get Organised | STEP 2

❏ You're in big trouble. Your income is not even covering your essential expenses. This means your finances are in really poor shape. In this situation you need to somehow increase your income by getting another job, or lower your essential expenses. You could do this by moving into a small house, where you may have less rent or smaller mortgage repayments to make each month.

> **A budget can show you exactly where you can change your spending habits.**

Step by step guide to budgeting

When creating a budget, try not to over or under-estimate your expenses or sources of income. Be realistic. There is no point in setting yourself unrealistic savings goals because you will only be discouraged when you can't achieve them.

Step 1   Create your budget according to your pay period, whether it's weekly, fortnightly or monthly.

Step 2   On one side of the page list all your sources of income for, say, a month (if that's your pay period), everything from your salary to government benefits and how much money your partner has agreed to give you in child support or spousal maintenance.

Step 3   Total the column at the bottom

Step 4   On the other side, list all your expenses for a month, and total that column. Include everything! Go through recent bills and work out the average monthly cost of things like utilities, your mobile phone bill and petrol. Make sure you divide quarterly bills, like council rates, by three to give you a monthly figure for your budget.

Women's Guide **To Going it Alone**

Step 5 Now take a look at the totals of the two columns and see whether or not you are over budget. If you aren't, look at how much money your can afford to save each month.

If you can't balance your budget, earning more income can be just as good as cutting expenses.

Now you've put all this time and effort into creating a budget, make sure you stick to it! This is really important if you're trying to get used to living off a lower income or running the family finances for the first time.

Get Organised | **STEP 2**

BUDGET PLANNER

TOTAL INCOME - TOTAL EXPENSES = AMOUNT YOU CAN SAVE

Type of Income	Amount Received Each Period
Salary after tax	$
Government payments	$
Child support and maintenance payments	$
Regular income from investments (eg rent, interest, dividends)	
TOTAL INCOME	$

Type of Expense	Cost Each Period
Household expenses	$
Debt repayments	$
Transport costs	$
Medical expenses	$
Education expenses	$
Personal expenses	$
Savings	$
Other	$
TOTAL EXPENSES	$

The following tables breakdown your expenses, and will help you calculate your total costs.

Household Expenses	
Groceries	$
Rent	$
Electricity	$
Water	$
Gas	$
Phone/Internet/Mobile	$
Pay TV (eg Foxtel)	$
Council Rates	$
Body Corporate fees	$
Repairs	$
Gardening/Cleaner	$
Furniture/Appliances	$
Home and contents insurance	$
Sub total	**$**

Debt Repayments	
Mortgage	$
Car loan	$
Credit card	$
Personal loan	$
Store card	$
Lay-bys	$
Sub total	**$**

Transport Expenses	
Petrol	$
Parking	$
Tolls	$
Car insurance	$
Car registration	$
Repairs/Services	$
Public transport	$
Taxis	$
Sub total	**$**

Medical Expenses	
Medical insurance	$
Doctor	$
Medicine/Contacts	$
Dentist	$
Optometrist	$
Sub total	**$**

Education Expenses	
School fees	$
University/TAFE fees	$
Text books	$
Uniforms	$
Camps/Excursions	$
Sport registration	$
Music/Dance lessons	$
Sub total	**$**

Personal Expenses	
Clothing and accessories	$
Hair cuts	$
Sub total	**$**

Savings	
Regular savings	
(holidays, special gifts etc)	$
Investments	$
Superannuation	$
Sub total	**$**

Other Expenses	
Life insurance	$
Income protection insurance	$
Child care	$
Child support payments	$
Sports and hobbies	$
Gifts	$
Movies, DVDs and entertainment	$
Eating out	$
Alcohol and cigarettes	$
Newspapers, magazines and books	$
Sub total	**$**

Jane had been brought up with a father working in the financial industry. He took care of all his family's money and bills. Her mother never had to worry about the family finances, as it seemed natural for her husband to do so. Jane thought this was the norm and left her family's finances to her husband too. She may have paid the odd bill, but found it all a bit hard. She was happy for her husband to handle everything, even though he had wanted her to help a bit more with the finances.

This continued after the break-up until the situation became complex, with money being moved around different accounts as their finances fell into disarray. Money had been a contributing factor in their arguments for a while, as they were often short of cash and credit was running high.

Jane, working as a casual teacher, found her access to their combined funds drying up and had trouble paying for groceries with her credit card, let alone having enough spending money. She had to keep asking her husband for more money and was often denied. It was then that she became pro-active with her finances. She put all her wages into her own account and taught herself, with some help from her dad, to run a budget.

IF YOU RECONCILE…

Separation doesn't always mean divorce. Time apart may help you and your partner remember what you love about each other, and before you know it everything goes back to normal.

To protect yourself against disaster, if you separate again down the track, there are a few things you should do.

Put together a contingency plan

To avoid a bitter separation down the track, enter into a binding legal contract that sets out a fair division of assets. If you do this while you are still happy, you have a good chance of getting what you really want.

A Binding Financial Agreement has to be prepared by a lawyer and signed by both you and your partner. A certificate of legal advice is also required to show that you both obtained independent legal advice on the matter.

At a cost of around $1,000, an agreement is much cheaper than a typical Family Court divorce hearing costing anywhere from $20,000 plus.

> **Separation doesn't always mean divorce.**

In your agreement you can also cover issues like how your children would be accommodated, who gets what property and furniture, and superannuation and retirement issues.

While an agreement like this is not that romantic, the reality is you have separated once already, what's to say it will not happen again.

Do not take on too much debt

You may feel like a young married couple again, but unless you effectively manage your financial situation things could turn sour.

Don't max out your credit cards on expensive family holidays celebrating your reunification. Don't allow your partner to take out any big loans, even if they are for the family business. If you blindly put your name to a couple of 'sign here' tags and the investment goes sour, you may lose your house.

As you consciously try and avoid getting into debt, you should also try and pay off existing debts. When you receive your financial statements showing all income and outgoings decide how much you can afford to pay off existing debts each pay period.

Keep track of all money coming in and going out

If you didn't pay much attention to your bank statements before you and your partner separated, make sure you read them all now you are back together.

Look at how much income is coming into the family each month and make sure it exceeds your expenses. If it doesn't you need to speak with your partner. Are there non-essential expenses you can cut down on, like alcohol and gym memberships? Or are there ways in which you could increase the family's income, like renting out the flat above the garage or one of you getting an extra job?

If you find any expenses that you are not sure about, you should also quiz your partner. There have been instances where some partners have built up their own kitty in a secret bank account, so they wouldn't have to share the money with their partner in the event of a divorce.

It might be a bit impractical to organise joint signatories for your every day account, but you could do this for your investment accounts. That way your partner is not able to withdraw any money without your consent.

Create a documents box

When you and your partner move back in together, make sure you find out where all your important documents are. This includes things like property deeds, share certificates, life insurance policies, and wills. From now on store them all in the one place, so you can keep track of them.

Women's Guide **To Going it Alone**

Get a job

If you don't already have a job, it's a good idea to try and get one. Not only will it increase the family's income, and take financial pressure off your marriage, but it also gives you some financial independence in case you separate again.

STEP 3

WHAT YOU'RE ENTITLED TO

Women's Guide **To Going it Alone**

STEP 3 | What You're Entitled To

The courts can rule on almost anything. They can deal with property purchased during the marriage, superannuation, gifts and inheritances, property owned before the marriage, assets and goodwill that's been built up in a business, compensation awards, lottery winnings, and even redundancy packages. The courts can also determine whether your partner should still provide you with financial assistance.

A leading financial planner we spoke with says very few husbands believe they have to divide their assets 50/50. They often think they just have to give their wife a bit of money so she can get by. That is NOT the case. In many settlements the assets are split so the wife gets at least 50/50.

DIVIDING THE ASSETS

The property settlement is the term used for who gets what after the end of a marriage; it's not just the house. The property the Court considers must have a connection to the marital relationship.

The Federal Magistrates Court can deal with property matters if the assets are worth less than $700,000, or if they have the consent of both you and your husband if your assets are worth more than that amount.

When you apply to the Court for orders about property you have to tell them everything about all of your property and financial assets. If you don't disclose everything, an agreement or orders that are made can later be set aside or varied.

If you and your husband agree on how your property should be divided without Court action, you can then apply to the Court for consent orders to formalise the deal. Consent orders are legally binding and are only granted if the Court is satisfied they are properly drafted and the terms are fair. An agreement can be reached at any time, even if proceedings have been started in the court.

Negotiating the settlement

The following documents will help your lawyer negotiate a settlement or instruct a valuer:

- ❏ Income tax returns and financial statements for both you and your partner and all associated entities and super funds

- ❏ Details of any super policies including fund name, the date the member joined the fund, and the member number

- ❏ The accountant's working papers

- ❏ Any budgets or forecasts

- ❏ Business Activity Statements

- ❏ Copies of Fringe Benefit Tax returns

- ❏ Copies of trust deeds, partnership agreements, and shareholder agreements

- ❏ Details of salary packages

- ❏ Schedules of any accrued leave entitlements

- ❏ Details of all cheque and savings accounts

- ❏ Ledgers of particular relevant accounts, for example loan accounts

- ❏ Bank statements

- ❏ Copies of insurance documents

- ❏ Asset schedules and any recent valuations

- ❏ Copies of any lease agreements

What You're Entitled To | STEP 3

If you have a business:

- ☐ Details of work in progress, including details of the ten largest current customers of the business

- ☐ Details of stock on hand and recent stocktake reports

- ☐ The names of creditors and debtors as at the date of the preparation of the last set of financial statements

- ☐ Loan application for any type of financing for business purposes, including all correspondence relative to any application

The number of years you will need to go back into the past will depend on the facts of the particular case. A good starting point is to have at least the last three years of published financial records.

Tax issues

Before you can agree on a financial settlement you need to consider the tax implications. Sit down with your partner and your accountants and determine the value of your assets after tax and the best way to split them. WHK Horwath says you and your partner have to work together if you want to minimise your tax. If you don't, the tax consequences can be a bit grim.

After your settlement is finalised you will get access to capital gains tax relief. That allows you to transfer assets from one partner to the other without incurring capital gains tax (CGT). For example, in normal circumstances, if a property other than your primary residence is sold you would have to pay tax on any gains you have made (the sale price minus the price you initially paid for the property). But if a property is transferred from your partner to yourself under a court order or binding agreement in a divorce proceeding, no capital gains tax has to be paid. The reasoning is that having to pay CGT on the transfer of assets in a divorce may affect the settlement. If you change the ownership of property before the courts formalise your settlement you will not be entitled to capital gains tax relief.

You also get stamp duty relief when transferring assets. This means if your partner transfers the family home or other property to you it's not like a regular purchase, so you don't have to pay any stamp duty.

It is really important you are aware of the tax implications when transferring assets held in certain legal structures. WHK Horwath says many people have assets in a company, assets in a super fund, or assets in a trust. When they get divorced they don't think of it like that, they think the assets are theirs…but actually they are the company's, the super fund's and the trust's. You need to deal with each asset within its legal structure, because that's what the tax office looks at.

Making the agreement stick

Once you have reached an agreement with your partner, you need to work out how you can make it stick. There are two main options, a financial agreement or consent orders.

Financial Agreement

A financial agreement is a binding legal agreement covering the financial settlement and financial support that one spouse makes to the other after the marriage. This is a legally binding agreement and must be signed by you and your spouse. You must receive independent legal advice before signing on the dotted line. Binding agreements may not be as secure as court orders, as there are more ways to set the agreement aside. It is a fairly technical agreement, so if you get anything wrong it may not be valid.

Consent Orders

A consent order is a written agreement that is approved by the Court and has the same effect as a court order, but you don't actually have to go to Court. Consent orders can cover the transfer of property, superannuation and maintenance. Watts McCray Lawyers consider court orders to be an easier, faster and more secure way to cement your agreement for many people. Another advantage of a court order is it is really hard to break or set aside. The Court endeavours to keep its orders in tact.

The costs of both financial agreements and consent orders are pretty similar and they are relatively simple to implement.

With both you get stamp duty relief when transferring assets. This means if your partner transfers the family home to you it's not like a regular purchase, so you don't have to pay any stamp duty.

You also get capital gains tax rollover relief, meaning you can transfer assets to the other partner without incurring capital gains tax at that time. For example, in normal circumstances, if a property other than your primary residence is sold you would have to pay tax on any gains you have made (the sale price minus the price you initially paid for the property). But if a property is transferred from your partner to yourself under a court order or binding agreement in a divorce proceeding, no capital gains tax has to be paid at that time. The reasoning is that having to pay CGT on the transfer of assets in a divorce may affect the settlement.

The Court's powers

Section 79 of the Family Law Act gives the Court very wide powers to redistribute your combined property.

You must receive independent legal and financial advice before signing on the dotted line.

You may have heard things from friends before like, 'if you have the kids 60 percent of the property should come to you' or 'since your kids are over 18 everything will be split 50/50'. But the Family Court emphasises the way your assets will be shared between you and your husband will depend on the individual circumstances of your family. It warns your settlement will probably be different from others you have heard about.

The Family Court doesn't use a formula to divide your assets. The decision is made after all the evidence is heard and the judge decides what is fair based on the unique facts of your case.

The Family Court will divide your assets based on:

- What you have got and what you owe
- Direct financial contributions to the marriage, like salaries
- Indirect financial contributions, like gifts and inheritance from families
- Non-financial contributions to the marriage like looking after the kids and homemaking

The Court also considers things like property owned at the time of marriage and effort put into running a business.

The Court can divide your assets in two ways. The most common 'global approach' looks at the total value of all your assets. For shorter marriages the Court make use the 'asset by asset approach', and look at you and your partner's interest in individual assets or property.

Test Cases

In Marriage of Norbis (1986) (10 Fam LR 819) the High Court decided that either approach is legitimate. In this case, the couple had been married for nearly 30 years and had a number of properties. The trial judge adopted the approach of isolating individual items of property. The High Court stated that; "which of the two approaches [the global or asset by asset] is the more convenient will depend on the circumstances of the particular case. However, there is much to be said for the view that in most cases the global approach is the more convenient."

Don't worry if you haven't made much of a financial contibution to the marriage because you have been raising your children. In many marriages the Court sees contributions by the homemaker and the income earner as equal. So don't underestimate your side of the bargain.

The Court looks at contributions made by each party to the well-being of the family. This includes things like looking after your kids, cooking meals, and ironing shirts. The Court will consider what impact this had on the earning capacity of your partner. Were they able to spend more time in the office, climbing the corporate lader, because you had everything covered on the home front?

> **Test Cases**
>
> In Marriage of Rolfe (1977) (5 FAM LR 146) Evatt CJ found the purpose of assessing contributions made by each party to the welfare of the family; "is to ensure a just and equitable treatment of a wife who has not earned income during the marriage, but who has contributed as a homemaker and parent to the property. A husband and father is free to earn income, purchase property and pay off the mortgage so long as his wife assumes the responsibility for the home and the children."
>
> In Marriage of Mallett (1984) (9 Fam LR 449) Wilson J argued "the contribution must be assessed, not in any merely token way, but in terms of its true worth to the building up of the assets… It is a wide discretion which requires the court to assess the value of that contribution in terms of what is just and equitable in all the circumstances."

Women's Guide — To Going it Alone

It is important to note that you and your partner won't automatically end up with the value of property you owned before the marriage, you may get less or more. One spouse may have brought property to the relationship, but it is assumed that over time both spouses contributed, directly or indirectly, to its maintenance and improvement. The longer the marriage, the less important pre-marriage ownership becomes .

> Sarah and her husband had grown apart over the years. They had made it to eighteen years of marriage and had two children, both in their teens. She was happy enough to potter along as they were, without many expectations and no limitations on her husband's work or leisure pursuits…of which there were many.
>
> Sarah had always worked part-time as an occupational therapist, mainly for interest rather than extra income. This was interrupted by periods of living in various parts of Asia, as her husband's work dictated. Living overseas was something she found very challenging, yet was prepared to do in order for the family to be together.
>
> It came as a huge shock when her husband announced that he planned on leaving the family and didn't want to try any form of counselling to work things out. He didn't have a new partner, he just wanted 'freedom'. Something Sarah didn't realise he was without. She says "he described it as not wanting to grow old with me".
>
> Sarah stayed in their substantial family home with the children for eighteen months after he shifted into an apartment. He had always taken care of the finances, despite Sarah offering to help pay the bills, which continued after their separation.

What You're Entitled To | STEP 3

> Sarah says she wishes she had been more pro-active in choosing a solicitor. She went with a recommendation and found the very capable, slick, young male lawyer a bit brash and the experience somewhat threatening. He was pushy and wanted Sarah to go harder on her husband, to get more out of him. But Sarah does not like confrontation and thought it was wrong, so resisted his insistence. That kept them out of the courts and helped relations with her husband.
>
> When it came time to have a financial settlement, Sarah and her husband split all property 50/50. She was found to have made a significant non-financial contribution to the marriage. She cared for their children, looked after the home, and moved the family overseas to support her husband's carer.
>
> Not going with the 'revenge angle' brought a financial settlement that much quicker. It also left the channels of communication open, which Sarah says is vital when you are co-parenting kids.

Going to court

You should arrive early, find your name on the list and then sit outside the courtroom until the court officer calls the name of your case.

When you go into the courtroom sit at the bar table facing the judge. An actual divorce hearing usually only takes a few minutes if all procedural requirements have been met.

If a lawyer is representing you, you don't have to say anything in court. If you don't have a lawyer, the judicial officer will ask you to state your name, the name of the respondent and any children under 18 years of age.

If you and your partner don't have any children, you are not required to go to court.

A full five-day property settlement hearing costs around $50,000. The Family Court hands down common sense solutions, but a small percentage of people will never agree with the decision.

EVERYDAY ASSETS

The Court will work out who gets what money and property. You and your partner have to follow its order.

If you are divorcing at a younger age, you and your husband are more likely to have to sell everything and then split the money. That's because you generally don't own enough assets to simply divide them up. For example, few 30 year olds own their house outright, let alone other investment properties or share portfolios. Meanwhile, if you are divorcing in your 50s, you may have enough assets to divide. For example, one person may take the family home and the other superannuation and a share portfolio worth a similar amount.

The house

The family home is often in the husband's name, but this doesn't mean it goes to him if the marriage breaks down. The Court is able to give the wife all or part of the house no matter what.

If there are sufficient other assets or a big superannuation entitlement the Court may give one person the home, especially if they have the children for most of the time. The other partner would then get the other big assets.

If you and your husband have no other substantial assets besides your home, the Court may order for it to be sold and for you to split the proceeds. The Court may put off the sale and let the parent looking after the kids full-time stay in the home until the children are grown up. You and your husband would both have to agree on this arrangement first.

After looking at what you and your husband contributed to the marriage, the Court will also look at your future requirements before handing down its order. It will take into account things like age, health, financial resources, care of children, and your ability to earn an income. The Court will also consider how much it costs to maintain the house.

Other assets

The Court treats other everyday assets like the family home. Things like cars, boats and holiday houses are valued. The Court then decides if they will be sold and the money split between you and your husband, or if you should divide them based on each person's interest in the asset. For example, you might get the family car and house and your husband might get the superannuation lump sum and the boat.

Remember anything that is of significant value can be part of the settlement. This includes everything from frequent flyer points to furniture.

While we're on the subject of furniture, this can be a really tricky asset to divide. The best thing to do is sit down with your partner early on in the separation and go through all your furniture. See who really wants what and whether you can agree on that. If you can't, the Court takes a pretty brutal approach on this. They will get you to do to a list of all your furniture and fittings and roughly divide them into two equal piles. One person can pick a pile, the other gets the remaining pile. Alternatively you can do a list of furniture and each person gets an alternate pick. For example, you pick one, he picks the next and so on.

When dividing furniture go for things that you really want, not things that you don't want but you don't want him to have. For example, don't take his dead mother's vase which you hate, just so he can't have it.

Gifts

The person who received a gift does not automatically get to keep it. They are treated like any other family asset.

The Court sees gifts as a contribution to the marriage. Like property, the longer the marriage the less important individual ownership is. It may seem hard to believe, but this even applies to family heirlooms. Just because something belonged to your family doesn't necessarily mean you'll get it.

> The real trial for Sarah came in the form of sorting out their individual possessions. Her husband, being a very organised person, had compiled a list of what he wanted.
>
> They moved around the house, room by room, listing what they had brought to the marriage and then saying what they wanted. This was the hard part. A few things they both wanted, even though he had never acknowledged them before.
>
> Sarah's husband used the passive bullying she had come to expect from him. "It was a power thing", Sarah says. By manipulating the situation he got what he wanted.

De-facto property

There is no national regime covering the division of property following a de facto relationship. Property isn't just your home; it's any real estate you own, investments, cash and even debt.

In most states it is the Local, District and Supreme Courts which deal with property disputes between de facto couples, not the Family Court.

If you were in a de-facto relationship that has broken down, you have two years from the end of the relationship to make an application to the Courts. In South Australia you have just one year.

What You're Entitled To | **STEP 3**

The Courts divide your combined property based on each partner's contribution to the property. Like a divorce order, this also takes into account both financial and non-financial contributions that each partner makes.

> Diane and her husband had been married for six years before he met another woman, with whom he had an affair. They had two young daughters, aged four and two years, and were paying off a mortgage on a house in middle-class suburbia. Diane is a trained teacher, but was a full-time mum at that stage.
>
> It took Diane a few years to "come out the other end" of feeling sad at being abandoned. The effect on their children was dramatic, though not long term. The toddler suddenly went back to crawling when her father moved out of home, and the four year old took on the role of caring for mummy. When Diane didn't appear as sad, her eldest went back to being a little girl and the two year old went back to walking.
>
> Both she and her husband looked after their money, with Diane paying the bills. Neither of them worried too much about the outgoings, as they always managed to get by. Diane had an understanding of finances from her upbringing, but it wasn't until she was forced to handle the day-to-day household finances that she fully grasped the idea of budgeting.
>
> Her husband gave her a regular amount each month that she then used to pay for everything, including the mortgage. Her dad taught her how to keep a budget, as he was an accountant. Diane found she quickly got into the habit of spending the same amount at the supermarket each week, rather than allowing some weeks to creep up on the extras. This made it easier to maintain her budget.

Diane's husband was happy for her to stay in their family home while they were separated for the first year. But after getting advice about how much he needed to pay, based on his income, he reduced his family payments.

The trouble for Diane was she desperately wanted to keep her girls in their original home. This led her to seek help from the government, which she found a harrowing experience. While they weren't rude, she felt like "a second class citizen", she explains. They were very efficient, but not caring about her changed circumstances and how foreign this process was for her. They found she was eligible for some benefits, which helped on a daily basis but didn't solve the on-going problem of needing to pay out her husband for his share of their house. Diane found it hard not to be bitter, "he wanted to have his cake and eat it too", she felt with growing anger.

Diane then turned to her bank to see if they could lend her the money she needed to buy her husband out of the family home, but with only the prospect of a teacher's part-time income, they didn't want to know her. Relying on family can be a blessing. Diane's father helped her pay a settlement to her soon to be ex-husband, who was happy to take a monetary share of the household goods rather than anything physically. They had a real estate agent come to value their property to determine an appropriate buy-out price.

When it came time to find a solicitor, Diane went to one in her area that she didn't know. This experience worked well. The solicitor gave her legal advice about organising the financial settlement, then a friend recommended someone who saw her through the legal proceedings of the divorce. The experience was one of loneliness, Diane explains, "but I felt brave at the same time that I could do this".

BANK ACCOUNTS

You need to make sure you are aware of all of the bank accounts you and your husband hold.

Legally, your husband can't set up a secret account and transfer money into it in the months leading up to your separation.

The Court requires both you and your husband to tell them about all of your property and financial resources. If everything isn't disclosed, any agreements or orders that are made can later be set aside or varied.

When the Court attempts to work out how to split a couple's property, they also take into account how much money is in bank accounts and the debt on credit cards. Generally, the money in everyday bank accounts is not very much in the scheme of things. It is the cash used to pay for everyday expenses, and is not for your long-term financial security. In some cases this money just offsets the debt on the credit cards.

Set up your own account

When the settlement is finalised, your bank accounts will not be tied to your husband's. You will have to go out and set up your own bank accounts.

How bank accounts work

Banks are the major receivers and lenders of money in the financial system. We deposit our money into savings accounts at a certain bank, where they pay us interest as a reward for choosing their bank. The bank combines the money from its deposit accounts to lend to other people at a higher rate of interest than the rate they pay out. That's how they make money.

The main types of accounts are savings accounts and cheque accounts, although these days the lines are blurring.

Savings accounts

Savings accounts are places to save or keep your money. Wages are usually paid directly into savings accounts. You can then access the money to pay for your everyday expenses.

> **Checking your statements also allows you to see exactly where your money is going ...**

Savings accounts usually pay very low rates of interest because the money in your account is 'at call', meaning you can withdraw any or all of your money whenever you want.

With these types of accounts you get a statement, either monthly or quarterly, listing your transactions. It's a good idea to check your statement and make sure all the transactions that are listed are correct. If you find an error, notify the bank and they can look into it for you. Checking your statements also allows you to see exactly where your money is going, which will help you with budgeting.

You can make deposits and withdrawals from your savings account either by filling out a form and handing it over the counter at the branch, using your debit card at an ATM, or transferring money and paying bills via internet or phone banking. Most financial institutions will charge higher fees for transactions that are made inside the branch and lower fees for transactions made online or through an ATM belonging to your branch. Banks are trying to encourage customers to use the machines rather than take up the time of banking staff.

Cheque accounts

A cheque is basically an instruction from you to your bank, telling them to take out a certain amount of money from your account and give it to the person whose name is on the cheque. All major banks offer cheque accounts.

Cheque accounts are handy because you have a record of all the payments you make on the cheque butts that are left in your chequebook, cheques can be sent by mail, and they are safer to carry around than cash.

What You're Entitled To STEP 3

There are disadvantages though. Some banks charge fees for keeping and operating the account, not everyone accepts cheques these days, and it takes a few days for cheques to clear and for the money to become available.

These days almost all bills can be paid using a plastic card, whether it be a card attached to your savings account or a credit card. It is worthwhile taking the time to consider whether you would get much use out of a cheque account. All accounts are subject to fees, charges and government taxes so it makes sense to only open accounts you really need. You may find you would rarely need to write out a cheque and it wouldn't be worth your while opening a cheque account.

If you don't have a cheque account, and you need to pay for a one-off expense with a cheque, there are other options. You can purchase a bank cheque from the bank. A bank cheque can be written by the bank, which you pay for with cash or money from your account. Bank cheques are often required when large purchases are made, for example, when buying a car. People feel safer accepting a bank cheque, rather than a large sum of money or a personal cheque, and it's treated just like cash.

Another alternative to a cheque is a money order, which can be bought at the post office. Money orders operate the same way as a bank cheque. The post office writes you out a 'cheque', for a maximum of $1,000, that you pay cash for. Australia Post charges a $4 fee for money orders.

These days many banks have a simple transaction account, which offers both ATM cards and a cheque facility. When you use an ATM you reach this account by selecting the 'savings account' option, rather than the 'cheque account' option.

Women's Guide To Going it Alone

Shop around for a bank account

It may be easier to go with the bank that your old accounts were with, but you should use this opportunity to shop around and check you are getting the best deal.

It can be really hard trying to decide which bank has the best accounts for you, because there are so many different types of accounts. The major things to look at when shopping around for an account are the differences between charges and interest rates from bank to bank. For example, some banks will let you make a certain number of transactions each month without incurring a fee. After you reach that limit, you will then have to pay for each additional transaction you make that month.

All this means it is a good idea to do your research and find out which bank offers the services, the type of account, and the system of fees and charges that you really want and that best suits you and your situation.

There are lots of different accounts, and banks call their products different names. The best ways to find out about the accounts is to walk into various banks and collect some brochures, speak to customer service officers, check out their websites or phone their information lines.

When comparing the various accounts of different banks, find out the answers to these questions:

- ❏ How much interest does each bank offer?
- ❏ What bank charges and account-keeping fees do you have to pay?
- ❏ How many free transactions can you make per month?
- ❏ How much will it cost you to use another bank's ATM?
- ❏ Does their account have a chequebook option?

What you need to open an account

Once you have decided which bank you will be opening your account with, just walk into a branch and the staff will help you.

When you go to open a bank account, you will need to prove who you are. This is usually done on a points system, under which things such as your passport, driver's licence, birth certificate and credit cards are worth a certain amount of points each. Generally, you must take in enough items to total 100 points. You will also be asked for your tax file number, so remember to take it with you.

You can open an account over the phone or the internet, but this can take longer as you still need to go into the branch anyway to show your ID and finalise it.

You can now open an online account with online banks, like ING Direct, over the Internet if you already hold a bank account with another lender. You simply go to the online bank's website and follow the prompts through the application process. You will need to provide them with your tax file number and the number (including BSB) of the account you hold with the other bank.

Automatic transfers

Once your property settlement has been finalised and you have set up a bank account, you can organise for any spousal maintenance or child support payments to be automatically transferred into your transaction account from your partner's.

All you need to do is give your BSB and account number to his bank. He then has to fill in and sign some forms to authorise the automatic transfer. A set amount will then be transferred into your bank account at a particular time of the month on a regular basis.

We will talk more about spousal maintenance later this chapter and about child support in Step 4.

Credit cards

When your divorce is finalised you will also have to apply for new credit cards. If you use your credit card sensibly, it can be a cheap and very convenient way of buying things. But if you make the mistake of over-using it when you can't afford to make repayments, you will end up with a huge debt.

When a bank agrees to give you a credit card it also advises you of your credit limit. The credit limit is the maximum amount of money the bank is willing to allow you to spend on credit. Each month you receive a statement listing all the things you bought and how much you have to pay back to the bank. Credit cards usually have an interest-free period, which runs for a specified period from when something is bought till the time when interest begins to be charged on the purchase. Each monthly statement has a 'due by' date. To avoid paying any interest you need to pay off your credit card debt each month. If you only make the minimum repayment, you will be charged interest on the rest of your bill.

Used unwisely, credit cards can get you into serious financial trouble. If you don't have the cash to pay for something now, and can't foresee that you will have the cash in a month's time when the bill is due, you shouldn't use a credit card. Eventually the bank will want you to pay them back and, until you do, they will charge you interest at quite a high rate on the amount you owe.

Choosing a credit card

When you are trying to choose a credit card there are a few major traps to watch out for. Make sure you find out:

- ❑ The rate of interest you will be charged

- ❑ The length of the interest-free period

- ❑ How much of the balance you have to pay back by the due date each month

- ❑ If the card has an annual fee and a higher interest rate, with a 55 day interest-free period after purchases, or if the card has lower interest rates and no fees, but a shorter interest-free period

- ❑ If the card charges interest from the date of purchase or from the date the statement is issued

Golden rules

- ❑ Always remember to read the terms and conditions of the credit card agreement. These are the rules you must abide by, and saying you didn't read them is no excuse.

- ❑ Don't let your credit card out of sight. It can be stolen or used for fraudulent purposes.

- ❑ If your card is lost or stolen, tell the bank immediately. That way the bank can put a stop on your card being used by someone else and minimise the chance your card will be charged with purchases you have not made.

- ❑ Memorise your PIN, don't write it down.

- ❑ If you are found to have contributed to any fraud through negligence with your card, you could have to pay for losses up to your credit limit. So follow the rules and keep control of your card.

- ❏ Check every credit card statement to make sure it is accurate. Sometimes errors occur and you may be charged for something you didn't buy. This might be the result of a simple clerical error somewhere along the line or it could be more serious. Other people may fraudulently use your credit card details to purchase things for themselves. If you suspect there is an error on your statement notify the bank straightaway so they can chase it up.

- ❏ Try not to over-use your credit card. You can get into serious debt if you aren't careful.

INVESTMENTS

Like your other assets, you need to track down all of your investments so they can be tallied up and divided fairly between you and your partner.

Are you across all investments?

The problem a lot of our divorced female friends have faced is that they just don't know what the couple has invested in. Over the years their husband has presented them with a piece of paper with a 'sign here' tag and that was that. There was no explanation of where there money was going, why the investment was selected, and what kind of returns it was expected to generate.

You need to dig up things like share certificates, managed fund details and deeds of any investment properties.

You and your husband are required to disclose all assets to the Court. This should prevent your husband from conveniently forgetting about an investment that you don't know about.

Understanding your investments

If you have never worked in the finance industry you may have limited knowledge of exactly what your investments are and how they work. Don't shut down when you hear terms like 'dividends' and 'managed funds'. Without your husband's guidance, you now need to learn how the finance world works if you want to ensure long-term financial security.

Shares

Buying shares is like buying part of a company. You become one of the owners. You make money when shares go up in price, and you sell, and when they pay a dividend. A dividend is your share of the profits and comes as cash.

If you have shares, your husband is likely to have invested across a number of industries to spread the risk. For example, if you invest in just resource stocks like BHP Billiton and Woodside Petroleum, you will lose money if there is a downturn in that sector. But if you own shares in a number of industries – like telecommunications, resources, retail, and banking – your returns will be much more balanced.

Managed funds

When you are in a managed fund you are still investing in the share market, you are just doing it with other people.

Managed funds are run by all the big financial institutions like Macquarie Bank, BT and AMP. You choose a particular fund, like growth, international equities, or balanced, and they pool your investment with other people's savings. Fund managers then manage that pool of money and choose where to invest it.

Investment property

An investment property is different from your house and your holiday house (if you are lucky enough to have one!). It is a property that has not been selected on its lifestyle merits, but its investment potential.

Investment properties are often units and are almost always rented out. They are located in areas that are expected to experience significant capital growth.

In Step 5 we explain these types of investments in greater detail.

Splitting the investments

You have the opportunity to try and reach an agreement with your husband on the division of investments before you go to court…but you shouldn't simply sell everything and split the cash. An investment isn't like a regular asset such as a car or a boat. Some investments should only be sold at certain times and others will charge you fees if you try to get out early.

Shares

If you plan to split your share portfolio, you need to make sure you get some advice from a stock broker or financial planner first. You can't just look at the market value of the portfolio and split it. You need to consider things like the future potential of the stocks. You don't want to be stuck with a bunch of shares that are fully priced, while your husband gets the ones with growth potential. You also need to make sure you get a portfolio of shares across a range of industries.

If you and your husband decide to sell all the shares at their current market price, and split the proceeds, you need to consider the tax implications. Every time you sell a share for more than you paid for it you make a capital gain, which you have to pay tax on. It may also be a bad time to sell some shares. For example, the company may have made a surprise announcement to the market that rattled investor confidence that day and the share price may recover in a week or so.

Managed funds

When you enter a managed fund you commit to pool your money for a certain period of time. If you pull out early you are unlikely to get the full benefit of the investment and you may incur exit fees from the fund manager. Exit fees may be a percentage of the money withdrawn or a flat fee.

> **You don't want to be stuck with a bunch of shares that are fully priced, while your husband gets the ones with growth potential.**

Investment property

When you look to sell your investment property there are also a number of fees that you will have to pay. If the sale price is greater than the purchase price, you may have to pay capital gains tax on the difference. You also have to pay for real estate agents and lawyers to execute the sale.

In some cases it is easier for you to tally up the value of all the assets and simply divide the actual investments, rather than sell everything and split the money. That way you don't incur exit fees and you don't jump out of an investment before it has reached its full potential. For example, one person could keep the investment property and the other any shares and money in managed funds.

Rebecca felt her husband Marty was very controlling and possessive, and decided a divorce was her only way out of an increasingly unhappy marriage.

They both wanted to stay out of the courts, so they froze their joint assets and enlisted the help of solicitors. Rebecca tried to keep their dealings amicable and proposed dividing their assets 50/50. Marty had other ideas. He didn't want to lose control of his wife and went through a few solicitors, pushing for them to try and wrangle a bigger share for him. Rebecca and Marty sold their family home and ended up splitting this evenly.

Marty owned a business that Rebecca wasn't involved in. She was frightened it would go bust and she would be liable for its debts by association. Rebecca offset this risk by accepting more cash and leaving Marty the investment property they owned. Her solicitor then put a clause in the divorce settlement that negated any financial responsibility for Marty's business.

When it came to divide their possessions, Marty dug in his heals as a way of being hurtful to Rebecca. He argued over everything of value, especially sentimental things, trying to score points emotionally against Rebecca.

SUPER

Laws introduced in 2002 allow superannuation to be split when a married couple divorce. This is really important, since super is often a family's second biggest asset...after the house.

The rules mean a family's superannuation assets are part of the mix, and the Family Court has more flexibility to divide assets fairly. It is important that a couple splitting superannuation assets gets professional advice and finds out exactly how much is in the super fund at the time of divorce. The social security system, the tax issues and the needs of the family must be considered. If the split is done carefully, it is possible for one partner to get part of the super assets and still get social security benefits to look after children.

Super is an incredibly important issue for women. The Association of Superannuation Funds estimates the average retirement payout for women in 2006 was $63,000. It estimates we need around $500,000 to have a comfortable lifestyle in retirement.

More women are part-time or casual workers and tend to be in lower-paid jobs. The problem is exacerbated by the fact women live longer and tend to be single as they grow older, due to divorce or widowhood.

How much super should you get?

When dividing up the family's assets do not underestimate the importance or the value of your superannuation. You need to contact the trustees of your super fund (if you have one) and your husband's fund and get all the relevant information. The most important thing is to find out how much it's all worth. You can get a form to do this from the Family Court.

When looking at how to split the super, the Court applies the same process as it does to other property. It can make an order to split funds in any percentage as long as it is just in all circumstances. The Court will again look at the financial and non-financial contributions you and your husband have made to the marriage. It will also take into account your future earning capacity.

If you husband's super is worth a lot more than your super, the Court may decide that you are entitled to more of other assets like the family home. This would mean you would get a greater share of the assets that are available to use now, but you wouldn't have any claim on your husband's super when you retire. As a result, your super retirement savings may be inadequate.

On the other hand, the Court may simply split the super lump sum in a certain way. If this is the case, you will need to set up your own super fund for this money to be transferred to.

In Step 5 we discuss the importance of setting up your own super fund.

Valuing super

To get your superannuation valued you have to request details about your super interests from the trustee of your super fund. Your accountant or lawyer can then use this information to determine the value of your super.

The valuation of super will depend on the type of interest and whether it is in a 'growth' phase or a 'payment' phase. In family law defined benefit funds are valued differently from other types of super.

Particular care has to be taken when splitting super interests in self managed super funds so capital gains tax rollover relief can be obtained.

De-facto

When it comes to superannuation, de-facto partners are not guaranteed the same rights as married couples. Laws allowing superannuation to be split when a couple divorce do not apply to de facto relationships.

The only way for a de facto spouse to receive all or part of their partner's superannuation is to be the nominated beneficiary in the event of their death.

FAMILY BUSINESS

You may not think of the family business as being part of the property settlement, but it is…and don't underestimate its worth.

Understanding your role

If either you or your husband started or ran the business and the other person did things like answer the phones, keep the books or entertain business associates, the Court will look at these efforts as a contribution to the business' success.

Even if you never worked in the business, but looked after the house or the children, you will be viewed as having made an indirect contribution. It was your efforts that freed your spouse to put time and effort into the business.

> ### Test Cases
>
> In Marriage of Whitely (1992) (FC) Rowlands J held that the wife was an inspiration of the husband's artistic and creative activities.
>
> In Marriage of Dawes (1989) (13 Fam LR 599) the Full Court of the Family Court recognised a wife's indirect contribution to her husband's business. It was found that the wife's indirect contribution to the business included her compliance in the operation of the business, her acceptance of a modest standard of living to allow business capital to be built up, her support of her husband's business decisions.

If you are a director or shareholder of the business, you hold a significant claim to the business and this shouldn't be treated lightly. If you are a director of the business, always seek professional advice; don't let your partner tell you your stake or position is worthless.

According to Watts McCray Lawyers, if your partner is the effective controller of the business and locks you out of the company, the Family Court can invoke laws which prevent your partner operating the business in certain ways and which require him to give you ongoing information about the business..

Your options

Deciding what to do with your directorship or shareholding is a big decision. You need to think about what role you are prepared to fill and whether your business is a good investment. Each situation is different.

If you are just going to be an inactive director, most lawyers would advise you to resign. You can still quit your directorship but retain your shareholding in the business. If you think you can contribute to the business, and work with your ex-partner, you may prefer to keep your post.

> **When transferring business assets you need to be aware of the tax implications.**

When you are trying to work out what to do with your stake in the business you need to need to determine whether or not it is a good investment and how much you would get for your shareholding if you sold it now. For example, if you and your ex-partner have an I.T. business, your stake may not be worth much now…but if you held on to it could be worth a lot in the future.

If you choose to sell your stake you need to remember your partner may not be able to afford to buy you out, but you could look for an alternative buyer.

If it is an amicable separation between you and your husband, you may decide to each take a 50-50 share of the businesses. That way nothing has to be sold, or taxed, and you get to keep the investment. If both you and your husband work in the business, and still get along, this could be a viable option.

If you need the Court to get involved and make a ruling on the business assets, they are going to do one of two things. The Court will either give one partner the whole business and the other something else of an equal value, like the family home. Alternatively the court will order for the business assets to be split 50-50. This doesn't just include the physical assets of the business, but also things like goodwill.

Depending on what your role is in the business, you shouldn't just consider keeping your stake or selling it. What about buying out your husband's stake with money from the property settlement?

When transferring business assets you need to be aware of the tax implications. According to Watts McCray Lawyers, if a transfer of assets is not structured properly Division 7A of the Income Tax Assessment Act can deem such a distribution to be a distribution of profits to a shareholder or associate. The tax effect could totally unbalance the fairness of the settlement.

You need to make sure you obtain good and early advice on this issue. In some cases, an asset split can be achieved without CGT and income tax being triggered, or at least the amount of tax payable can be significantly reduced. Speak to your accountant about how you can minimise this problem.

Business Partners

Things get a bit more complicated if there are other partners involved in the business. The Family Law Act now has significant powers against third parties. If your husband pretends his business isn't going well, rules aim to stop structures preventing a fair division of assets. For example, the court can force your husband's partners to buy his shares if he is claiming he doesn't have enough money to buy you out or give you an adequate share of the property settlement.

How to sell the stake

If you decide you want nothing to do with your stake in the family business, you have two options. You can see if your husband wants to buy you out or you can sell it to an outside investor.

You have to treat the sale of your business like you would a house. Before you start looking for a buyer, get things in order. This will help you get the highest price possible. Make sure you have up to date financial records, legal documents and information on how your business is run on a day-to-day basis. It also helps to have a detailed history of your business, along with any information on your competition and your industry. Also get the physical side of the business organised. Make sure the business premises are presentable and your equipment is up to date.

The next thing you need to do is have your business independently valued. There are a number of business brokers who specialise in this. You should also get an accountant, who has advised on and been involved in the operation of your business, to value it.

The most common way to value the business is to work out future maintainable earnings. This method looks at the expected future stream of profits from the business. It shouldn't be used if there's an inadequate history of earnings or if the business has low profitability or erratic past performance.

What if the business deals with a lot of cash, like a plumbing business or a shop? How do you work out the real profitability? Your husband is required to give full and frank disclosure. If you think cash is an important part of your husband's business and he is not revealing that, get your accountant to follow the cash trail.

Once you have a figure, put that to your husband and see if he wants to buy your stake. If not, you need to select a business broker who specialises in selling businesses and has experience in your industry.

FAMILY TRUSTS

Family Trusts are treated like part of the property settlement. The Court looks at what contributions have been made, how long you have been married, and what you brought in at the start of the union.

The Court then evaluates your future needs. Things like your earning capacity, care of small children and your health. The Court will then exercise its discretion when working out what's fair and reasonable.

Types of trusts

There are two main types of trusts, discretionary and unit trusts.

A discretionary trust is where you run it and decide how the money is distributed. The money can be split however you like between the beneficiaries, usually to get the greatest tax benefits. A trustee manages a family trust for the beneficiaries, who are normally extended family members. The trustee gets to decide which of the beneficiaries receive the fund's income and to what extent.

A Unit Trust is more like a company. Beneficiaries have units in the trust and profit is split accordingly. This is usually for a business of some sort.

Most trusts are used to split income and give it to your children to reduce tax.

Splitting trusts

While most family trusts can be broken in the Family Court, the Court is tougher on trusts than it used to be.

You need to talk to your solicitor and accountant before you apply to do this. You don't want to give up things like tax losses or benefits, but you may have to if you want to restructure the trust.

MAINTENANCE

According to the Family Law Act a person has a responsibility to financially assist their spouse if that person can't meet their own reasonable expenses. This does not change because of separation or divorce.

Divorce

Spousal maintenance is not automatic. The Court takes into account your needs and your husband's capacity to pay.

The Court will look at both you and your husband's; age, health, income, property, financial resources, ability to work, what is a suitable standard of living, if the marriage has affected your ability to earn an income, and who the children should live with.

Your earning capacity can be diminished, because of the relationship, even if you didn't have any children. You may have moved interstate or overseas because of your husband's job, and as a result had to put your career on hold. Or, your husband may have encouraged you to take on a less demanding position to help support him and his career.

To apply for spousal maintenance, complete and lodge an Application for Maintenance form with any office of the Family Court. On this form you will need to outline exactly what orders you want the Court to make. If you don't have any proceedings in the Family Court, apply to the Federal Magistrates Court.

Proceedings for spousal maintenance have to commence within 12 months of your divorce becoming final. Your spousal maintenance will usually stop if you remarry or enter a new de-facto relationship.

In the past the Family Court was reluctant to make spousal maintenance orders, preferring to stick to making orders that separated the parties' affairs. Now, the Court is more willing to make a spousal maintenance order due to evidence women have a much lower standard of living after separation[2].

[2] *Barry Rosemary (ed), The Law Handbook, Redfern Legal Centre Publishing, NSW, 2004, pg. 655*

Permanent spousal maintenance is pretty rare. Instead, maintenance is often granted for a few years while you retrain or are given more assets to make up for your lower earning capacity.

A leading financial planner we spoke with says you are better off trying to get more in the financial settlement than relying on getting a regular cheque from your husband. Go to him and say this is what we have today, and I'm going to take this now. You don't want any uncertainties.

Remember we are just talking about spousal maintenance here, not child support. We discuss that later in Step 4.

> Rebecca and Marty were able to agree on a settlement, through their solicitors, and avoided intervention by the courts. They had no children together, so child support was not an issue.
>
> Marty ran his own business and Rebecca was a successful accountant. Both spouses were able to support themselves financially, so it was agreed no spousal maintenance would be paid.
>
> Rebecca feels the separation and divorce process was much easier because children weren't involved. They had a cat that Marty decided he had to have and pushed for until Rebecca weakened and gave in. In the end the cat ended up with his parents!
>
> Rebecca feels she went in as aggressively as possible to get what she wanted. She knew she only had herself to worry about and it didn't matter if she ever saw Marty again. Rebecca's father ended up as the go-between as communication broke down with Marty. She knew this put a toll on her father, but it was the only option and at least Marty still spoke with him.

De-facto relationship

Different rules apply to de-facto relationships.

Limited spousal maintenance rights are only available in New South Wales, Tasmania, Western Australia, the Northern Territory and the ACT. They are not available in Victoria, Queensland and South Australia.

In the ACT, NSW and the Northern Territory you have to prove you are incapable of supporting yourself adequately because either you are caring for children from the relationship or your earning capacity was reduced as a result of the relationship. If the latter is the case, you need to propose to do a course or training to increase your earning capacity.

In Tasmania, you only need to establish that you are unable to support yourself for reasons connected with the relationship.

STEP 4

PROVIDING FOR YOUR CHILDREN

Women's Guide | **To Going it Alone**

Providing For Your Children | **STEP 4**

REACHING AN AGREEMENT

If you and your partner can't agree on decisions about your children's future, family and child mediators and counsellors can help you resolve your differences and reach an agreement.

Parenting plans

There are three basic issues that you and your partner have to deal with. You need to work out where your children are going to live, what contact they are going to have with each parent and how they are going to be financially supported. You can either put together an informal plan or choose to register a set plan with the Family Court. To do this you need to get form 26A and complete the steps.

Consent orders

Consent orders are made when your and your partner want your parenting plan to be legally binding.

You both need to take a signed copy of the parenting plan and file a form 12A in the Court. The plan is reviewed and then stamped with the court seal and sent back to you.

Consent orders are Court orders and are usually prepared by a lawyer. It is possible to put them together yourselves with the help of the Family Court's Consent Orders Kit.

Counselling

The Family Law Act encourages disputes involving children to be resolved through family and child counselling instead of going to court. Family Court counselling is free of charge.

In most cases the Court will only make an order if the parents have already seen a counsellor and were unable to reach an agreement.

Mediation

If you and your husband were unable to reach an agreement by yourselves or with the help of a counsellor, mediation is your last resort before heading to Court. This is not the same as counselling.

You can organise mediation through the Family Court. It usually takes two or three sessions to reach an agreement. This service is free.

Going to Court

If you and your partner still can't agree on an arrangement for your children, you can go to Court and apply for Parenting Orders. You can apply to either the Family Court of the Federal Magistrates Court for orders about parenting. The latter deals with less complex matters.

> **You can organise mediation through the Family Court.**

You and your partner need to do everything possible to avoid a legal battle. Not only is it very costly, it is also stressful and can take a long time.

If either parent is after something away from the norm, they are likely to be disappointed. The Court usually finds it best for the children if the new parenting arrangements make as few changes to their daily routine as possible.

Children generally don't have to physically go to Court. The Court can get information about the children from a counsellor, evidence from other people like teachers, or have the judge conduct a private interview with the children.

The Court considers contact with family members to be the right of a child, not the right of a parent. It generally finds it is in the best interest of the child to maintain contact with both parents.

According to section 68 of the Family Law Act, the Court will consider the following when making its decision:

- the relationship with both parents
- the wishes of the child and factors which might affect the weight they give to those wishes, for example how old the child is
- the effect on the child of any separation from a parent or other child
- the practical difficulty and cost of the child having contact with a parent
- the ability of each parent to care for the child
- the age, sex and cultural backgrounds of the child (including any need to maintain contact with Aboriginal or Torres Strait Islander culture)
- the need to protect the child from any physical or psychological harm caused by any abuse or violence
- the attitude of the parents to the child and to their parenting responsibilities
- any violence or violence order in the family
- whether the Court order will lead to further applications
- any other factors the Court thinks relevant

Court orders

There are a number of orders the Court can make. You have to accept them whether you like it or not. However, you have the right to appeal parenting orders.

Residence Orders

The Court gets to say who the child lives with. This person does not automatically have the right to make decisions about the child on their own. They will usually have to discuss decisions, on things such as education and holidays, with the other parent.

Contact Orders

These orders refer to the contact with the parent the child is not living with, and may cover contact with other people like grandparents. The order will specify how often and how long the contact will be.

Maintenance Orders

The Court can order how much child support should be paid and by which parent. Child support is basically money to cover the every day expenses of looking after your kids. It is different from spousal maintenance.

Child support is generally paid by the parent who does not live with the child full-time.

We go into child support in more detail later on this chapter.

Specific Issues Orders

The Court is also able to make orders about specific issues that are not covered by residence, contact or maintenance orders. For example an order may be made about the needs a child has, like taking medication, or the religious upbringing of a child.

Providing For Your Children | **STEP 4**

> Sarah, who we heard about in the last step, may have been manipulated by her husband when they were splitting up the assets…but she got what she treasured most and she gets to tuck them into bed every night.
>
> Custody was worked out between the two of them with their kids' best interests at heart, rather than their own self-interests. At no time did they have to attend a court, and both are grateful of that.
>
> The dynamics change after separation, with friends you'd seen as a couple suddenly disappearing, Sarah explains. This is hard to get used to but eventually you make a history for yourself as a single parent and old friendships are valued even more. She believes her husband feels he has missed out on not being with his children more often than just on weekends, but he would never admit to that.

Relocation

Relocation is a real issue in family law. It has been the source of complex litigation over the last few years, especially as the voice of men is increasingly heard in the Courts.

When you are working out a child support agreement, discuss what would happen if the parent who looks after the children full-time moves away from the other parent. Should the children automatically be able to go with their full-time carer? What if the move is simply because the parent with the kids can't afford to live in the city and has to move to a regional location?

Put your decision in writing in the agreement. If you then end up going to Court over this issue, they will take your agreement into account.

WHO IS FINANCIALLY RESPONSIBLE FOR YOUR CHILDREN?

The Family Law Act applies to all children. It doesn't matter whether their parents are married or not, or were never even in an on-going relationship together. Both parents, of a child under 18 years old, are responsible for the child. They both have a duty to look after them and provide financial support.

Child support system

Child support, or maintenance, is money paid by a parent who does not have sole daily care of a child or children to help cover their living expenses. It is payable until the child turns 18 years old.

Under the old system, to get child support or to change orders you needed to go to the Family Court. The old child support system still applies to situations where parents separated before 1 October 1989 and to every child of a relationship born before that date.

Under the current system, you apply to the Child Support Agency (CSA) for financial support, not the Court. This system looks after child support for children who were born on or after 1 October 1989, whose parents separated after that date, and children who have a sibling born after that date.

Child support can be arranged by private arrangements, child support agreements or CSA assessments.

Private arrangements

If you and your partner work out a private arrangement, the CSA or the Courts do not need to be involved.

Private arrangements give parents greater flexibility to decide how much money should be paid, how it should be paid, and how often payments should be made.

The CSA can provide you with specific information on how to work out the child support payable. The CSA website (www.csa.gov.au) has a calculator function you can use to get an estimate of how much child support should be paid.

A private arrangement is your best option if you do not want to get the CSA involved and if you receive only the base rate of the Family Tax Benefit or don't receive the Family Tax Benefit. If you receive more than the base rate of the Family Tax Benefit, Centrelink requires you to apply for an assessment by the CSA. We go into more detail about the Family Tax Benefit later on in this chapter.

It's a good idea to put your private arrangement down on paper, so there are no misunderstandings between you and your partner. If you want your private arrangement to be binding you need to register the level of child support with the CSA.

Child support agreements

Under child support agreements you and your partner make your own agreement on how much child support will be paid and how frequently. It must be in writing and signed by both parents. You then register the agreement with the CSA.

Under this option, you can either collect child support payments privately or ask the CSA to collect the payments and pass them on to you.

This agreement is considered to be a legal document, and can only be changed by a new agreement.

The CSA can't draw up an actual child support agreement for you. It does provide a child support agreement form, which you can use to help draw up your agreement. This form is available on the agency's website www.csa.gov.au. A solicitor would also be able to help you draw up an agreement.

CSA assessments

Under this option the CSA works out how much child support should be paid. It does this by using a legislative formula based on the care arrangements between you and your partner, as well as your income.

This formula takes into account things like each parent's income, the number of children you have, the living expenses of the parent, and the living arrangements.

The CSA will work out a parent's level of care based on the actual time the parent is looking after the child. This is usually based on the number of nights the parent will have responsibility of caring for the child in the 12 months immediately after the start of a child support period.

You can opt to either collect child support payments privately or ask the CSA to collect the payments and pass them on to you.

You can apply for a CSA assessment by calling the agency to make an application over the phone or by completing an Application for Child Support Assessment (paying parent) form.

Issues that can slow down the process of determining child support are paternity and correct income. If your partner is disputing the paternity of any child, the child support assessment by the CSA will be delayed while it conducts DNA testing. There may also be delays if you dispute your partner's income. For example, the income some businessmen and tradesmen put in their tax return is not their real income. If you think your assessment is wrong, you can make an appeal. This process takes three to six months. If you are still not happy you can go to the Family Court as a last resort.

Providing For Your Children | STEP 4

Make sure your child support arrangement covers everything. You don't want to be caught short when unexpected expenses pop up. Think about how much it costs to feed, clothe, house and entertain your children. Also consider whether you and your partner want to give your children extra things and who is going to pay for them.

Think about the schooling of your children, no matter how young they are. Do you want them to go to private schools? If so, who pays for that? You can't just calculate for school fees, but what about compulsory building fund donations, excursions, uniforms and expensive textbooks?

> **Make sure that your child support arrangement covers everything. You don't want to be caught short when unexpected expenses pop up.**

The same goes for things like private health insurance. You need to work out how much this costs each month and whether it should be added to child support payments.

Also discuss how a change in circumstances may effect your agreement. What if either of you find a new partner? What happens if one person loses their job? Or, on the other hand, gets a really big promotion and pay rise? And what happens if your child's circumstances change?

If you and partner can't reach an agreement on any areas of your child support arrangement, you can apply to the Court to help you resolve these issues.

Diane, who we heard about in Step 3, fortunately didn't need a formal custody or child support agreement regarding her two and four year old daughters. She was able to sit down with her husband and work out an arrangement that would suit their girls and was workable for them.

After twelve years they are still co-operating smoothly. Diane has remarried and given the girls, who their step-dad sees as his own, a hyphenated surname. Their school teachers even comment on how well adjusted the girls are and how you wouldn't know that they are from a divorced family situation.

The solicitor Diane saw advised her not to speak derogatively in front of the children about their natural father and what caused the break-up, instead wait until they were old enough to ask questions. At that point in time they could discuss it with their father and get information first hand.

With the friendliness lasting between the adults, maintenance was also not a big issue. Some money is paid towards the girls' up-keep, while their stepfather pays their school fees. He is happy to do this as it makes him feel pro-active in their upbringing too.

Diane feels that sometimes marriage break-ups are meant to be. In her case she has two lovely daughters and an adoring husband who she knows she was destined to be with.

HOW MUCH YOU ARE ENTITLED TO PER CHILD

Child support has to help you cover all the expenses you face in raising your children.

You need to think about all the costs you will incur and plan for them. Things like:

- Accommodation
- Food and clothes
- Extra curricular activities like dancing lessons and sports registration
- School fees
- School supplies like uniforms, books and stationery
- Transportation
- Health costs like health insurance and bills for doctors, dentists, optometrists, orthodontists and so on
- Holidays
- Pocket money
- Counselling
- Child care
- One off expenses like birthday presents, holiday camps and school excursions

Calculating child support

Child support is calculated using a formula. It takes into account each parent's income, the number of children, living expenses of the parents and the living arrangements of the children. The Child Support Agency says this formula means each assessment can be calculated fairly and accurately. It balances the interests of both parents and focuses on the needs and costs of their children.

Basic formula

From 1 July 2008 the CSA is using a new formula to work out how much child support should be paid. There are eight steps it uses to calculate child support for each child.

Step 1 Calculate each parent's child support income

Adjusted income − self-support amount = child support income

To get your adjusted income add your taxable income to any foreign income exempt from tax, rental property losses, and gross reportable fringe benefits for the relevant tax year.

The self-support amount for 2008 is $18,252. This amount is indexed each year.

Step 2 Add both parent's child support incomes together to get a combined child support income.

Step 3 Divide each parent's individual child support income by the combined child support income to get an income percentage.

Step 4 Work out each parent's care percentage of the child.

See the Child Support Care and Cost Table to determine their care percentage.

Child support payments will reflect each parent's level of care and how much it costs parents to care for their children. For example, if a paying parent has regular care of a child, their child support assessments are reduced to acknowledge they directly contribute to the costs of raising the child through care.

Step 5 Work out each parent's cost percentage of the child.

See the Child Support Care and Cost Table to determine their cost percentage.

Parents with regular or shared care will be acknowledged as directly meeting some of the costs of the children through care. For example, parents with regular care will be acknowledged as directly meeting 24 percent of the costs of the children. The remainder of their share of the costs is payable as child support.

Child Support Care and Cost Table   *Source: Child Support Agency*

Child support care (%)	Equal to no. of nights / year	Equal to no. of nights /fortnight	Care level	Child support cost (%)
0-13%	0-51 nights	1 night	Nil	Nil
14-34%	52-127 nights	2-4 nights	Regular	24%
35-47%	128-175 nights	5-6 nights	Shared	25% plus 2% for every % point over 35%
48-52%	176-189 nights	7 nights	Shared	50%
53-65%	190-237 nights	8-9 nights	Shared	51% plus 2% for every % point over 53%
66-86%	238-313 nights	10-12 nights	Primary	76%
87%-100%	314-365 nights	13-14 nights	Sole	100%

Step 6   Subtract the cost percentage from the income percentage for each parent. The result is called the child support percentage.

If it's a negative percentage, that parent may receive child support because their share of the costs of children is more than the amount of care they provide.

If it's a positive percentage, that parent needs to pay child support because they aren't meeting their entire share of the costs of the child directly through care. If a parent has a positive child support percentage they need to proceed to Steps 7 and 8.

Step 7   Work out the costs for each child.

Refer to the CSA's Costs of Children 2008 tables at the back of the book. An independent taskforce analysed the cost of children and compiled these figures.

Step 8   You get the final child support payable by multiplying the positive child support percentage by the costs of the child.

This final figure is the child support amount the paying parent needs to transfer to the other parent.

Source: www.csa.gov.au

I know this formula seems really complicated, but if you take time to go through it slowly, it actually makes a lot of sense. Try and follow this example.

Providing For Your Children | **STEP 4**

John and Sarah have separated and have a child support assessment. John's 2007-08 taxable income was $45,000. He also received $15,000 in foreign income. Added together his adjusted taxable income is $60,000. The self-support amount of $18,252 is deducted from his income. That gives him a child support income of $41,748.

Sarah's 2007-08 taxable income was $20,000. She also had a $5,000 rental property loss. Added together her adjust taxable income is $25,000. The self-support amount of $18,252 is deducted from her income. That gives her a child support income of $6,748.

Added together John and Sarah's combined child support income is $48,496. The income percentages show the portion of the costs of the children each parent should meet. For John, this is $41,748 divided by $48,496 – he needs to meet 86 percent of costs. For Sarah, this is $6,748 divided by $48,496 – she needs to meet 14 percent of costs.

John and Sarah's two kids, Jack and Jill, live with Sarah most of the time. They spend every second weekend and some school holidays with John. That gives John a regular care level of between 14 and 34 percent and Sarah a primary care level of 66 to 86 percent.

The Child Support Agency then works out the amount each parent directly contributes to the cost of the children through care. Based on their level of care, John has a cost percentage of 24 percent and Sarah has a cost percentage of 76 percent (see Child Support Care and Cost Table).

The cost percentage is then subtracted from the income percentage for each parent, to work out the child support percentage. For John this is 86 percent minus 24 percent, giving him a child support percentage of 62 percent. For Sarah this is

14 percent minus 76 percent, giving her a child support percentage of -62 percent.

Sarah's child support percentage is a negative number, so she may receive child support. According to the Child Support Agency her share of the costs of the two children is more than the amount of care she provides. John's child support percentage is positive, so he needs to pay child support because he isn't meeting his share of the costs of the children through care.

To determine how much child support John should pay, the costs for each child have to be considered. Jack is 8 years old and Jill is 10 years old. The table Costs of the Children 2008: Children aged 12 years and under (see the back of the book) needs to be used to work out how much it costs to raise them.

John and Sarah's combined child support income is $48,496. According to the table the cost to raise Jack and Jill is $6,571 plus 23 cents for every $1 of income over $27,378. The calculation is:

$48,496 minus $27,378 = $21,118

Multiply $21,118 by 23 cents = $4,857

Add $4,857 to $6,571 = $11,428

The cost of the two children is $11,428. Divide that by two, and the cost of each child is $5,714.

The final child support payable is calculated by multiplying John's positive child support percentage by the costs of the child. If you multiply 62 percent by $5,714 you get $3,542.

John has to pay Sarah $3,542 in child support per child per year.

Child support can be paid in a lump sum instead of regular payments. This is not very common and generally relates to people who can't afford or who won't pay regular child support. For example if one parent has a really large asset but no income. This might be sold, and part of the proceeds put into a child support trust to cover regular payments.

Still at high school

If your child turns 18 and is still at high school, don't worry about how you will look after them without child support or them earning an income. You can apply for an extension of your child support assessment until the end of the school year. You have to apply for an extension before the child turns 18, unless there are exceptional circumstances.

The Family Law Act specifically states the "Court must not make a child maintenance order in relation to a child 18 years and over unless the provision of maintenance is necessary to enable the child to complete his or her education".

Completing tertiary education

If your child is over 18 and is in tertiary education, you can apply to the Family Court for child support payments to continue.

Remember, your child is also able to apply to Centrelink for Youth Allowance. If they are 18, still living at home, and studying full-time they can receive $233.90 per fortnight. This is subject to income and asset tests.

GOVERNMENT SUPPORT

If you are struggling to support your children on the child support payments you receive from your partner, you can also apply for government support. However, the government only hands out benefits to those who really need it, so you will often be subject to an income test and an assets test.

An income test looks at how much you earn in a financial year. If you earn over a set amount, you won't be entitled to the government benefit because they figure you don't really need it.

An assets test looks at the value of what you own. It covers everything from your savings in the bank to the value of shares you own to your cars.

To get these benefits you must be an Australian resident.

Family Tax Benefit Part A

Family Tax Benefit Part A is an annual tax benefit aimed at helping families with the cost of raising children.

You can apply for this benefit if you have dependent children under 21 or a dependent full-time student aged 21 to 24.

To receive this benefit your income and the child support you receive must be below a certain amount. Contact Centrelink for more details.

The maximum rate of Family Tax Benefit A is:

For each child	Per fortnight	Per year
Under 13 years	$145.46	$4460.30
13-15 years	$189.00	$5595.45
16-17 years	$46.90	$1890.70
18-24 years	$63.00	$2310.45

www.centrelink.gov.au

Family Tax Benefit Part B

Family Tax Benefit Part B gives extra help to families with just one main income. This includes single parents.

You can receive this benefit if your youngest dependent child is less than 16 years old. You can also get the benefit if you have a 16 to 18 year old if they are a full-time student and don't receive Youth Allowance.

This benefit also gives extra assistance to families who have kids less than five years of age.

Single parents are not subject to an income test for this benefit.

The maximum rate of Family Tax Benefit B is:

Age of youngest child	Per fortnight	Per year
Under 5 years	$125.02	$3,259.45
5-15 years (or 16-18 years if full-time student)	$87.08	$2,270.30

www.centrelink.gov.au

Unlike Family Tax Benefit A, which you get per child, Benefit B is per family (meaning you can only get it once).

Parenting Payment

You may also qualify for a Parenting Payment if:

- ❏ You are single and have at least one child under 8 in your care (when the child turns 6 you will have part-time participation requirements)

- ❏ You are partnered and have at least one child under 6 in your care

To get this payment both your income and your assets have to be below a certain amount.

The maximum rate of Parenting Payment is:

Status	Maximum rate per fortnight
Partnered	$387.80
Single	$537.70

www.centrelink.gov.au

Child Care Benefit

You could also receive a Child Care Benefit if you use an approved or registered child care centre and have to pay fees. Your child must be immunised.

Approved Care

Approved childcare providers have been approved by the Australian Government to pass the Child Care Benefit straight on to families, and deduct it from their fees. Most long day care, family day care, before and after school care, vacation care, some in-home care and occasional care services offer approved care.

Centrelink says all families can get up to 24 hours of Child Care Benefit for approved care per child per week. If you and your partner are working or studying for at least 15 hours a week, you may be eligible for 50 hours of Child Care Benefit per child per week. Contact Centrelink's Family Assistance Office for more details. You will find the number at back of this book.

The Child Care Benefit payment can be paid directly to childcare service providers to reduce the fees you are charged. It can also be paid as a lump sum to you at the end of the financial year. The Child Care Benefit is subject to an income test, but not an assets test.

If your child is in approved care, you are entitled to the maximum Child Care Benefit if your annual family income is $35,478 or less.

Maximum rate of Child Care Benefit for non-school child in approved care:

Number of children in care	Per week (for 50 hours of care)	Per hour for each child
1	$168.50	$3.37
2	$352.17	$3.52
3	$549.63	$3.66

Maximum rate for a school child is 85 percent of the maximum non-school child rate.

www.familyassist.gov.au

Registered Care

Nannies, grandparents, relatives, some private pre-schools, kindergartens, occasional care centres and outside school hours centres are registered with the Family Assistance Office. You are only entitled to the minimum rate of Child Care Benefit if your kids are in registered care, not approved care.

Minimum rates of Child Care Benefit:

Per hour for each child	Maximum per week for each child (for 50 hours a week)
$0.564	$28.20

www.familyassist.gov.au

If you are using registered care, you can only claim your Child Care Benefit after you have already paid your fees. Lodge your childcare receipts at the Family Assistance Office within 12 months after the care has been provided.

Youth Allowance

Your child is able to apply for Youth Allowance if they are aged 16 to 24 and studying full-time. They may also be eligible for this benefit if they are aged 16 to 20 and looking for work full-time, and can prove it by meeting an Activity Test.

If your child is under 18, and hasn't completed their final year of school, they are generally required to be in full-time education or training to qualify for Youth Allowance.

Youth Allowance payments are subject to strict income and assets tests of your child, if they are considered to be an independent, or of you, if they are considered to be dependent. For more information contact Centrelink.

The maximum Youth Allowance payment rates for living at home are:

Status	Allowance paid per fortnight
Under 18, at home	$194.50
18 and over, at home	$233.90

www.centrelink.gov.au

Widow Allowance (Also for Divorcees)

As funny as it sounds, a Widow Allowance is not just for widows. It's basically for anyone who has lost their partner, whether it be through death or divorce.

You may be able to qualify for the government's Widow Allowance if you:

- Were born before 1 July 1955 and are single

- Have become a widow, divorced or separated since turning 40

- Have no recent workforce experience. This means you haven't worked at least 20 hours a week for 13 weeks or more in the last year

You can only receive the allowance if your income and assets are below a certain amount.

If you pass the requirements, and can receive the allowance, you have to attend an interview with a Personal Advisor at least once a year. At this interview the advisor can help you to develop a plan for getting a job or becoming more involved in the community.

The payment rates for the Widow Allowance are:

Status	Allowance rate per fortnight
Single, no children	$429.80
Single, with children	$464.90
Single, aged 60 or over	$470.70

www.centrelink.gov.au

Women's Guide To Going it Alone

Newstart Allowance

You may be eligible for the Newstart Allowance if you are having trouble finding a job. This is a fortnightly payment from the government to people who are actively looking for work. You can only receive this payment if your family income and assets are below a certain level. You have to be over 21 and under Age Pension age to qualify.

The payment rates for Newstart Allowance are:

Status	Allowance rate per fortnight
Single, no children	$429.80
Single, with children	$464.90
Single, aged 60 or over	$470.70

www.centrelink.gov.au

For more information on any of these benefits and to find out what you're entitled to, contact Centrelink.

STEP 5

INVESTING YOUR SHARE

Women's Guide **To Going it Alone**

When the property settlement is finalised you are likely to end up with a large amount of money that has to last you into retirement. To get the most from your money and really make it last, use a financial planner. They can help your work out the best investments for you, and manage them.

PAY OFF THE HOUSE

Achieving the Great Australian Dream of paying off your home would make your day-to-day living a lot more comfortable. Imagine not having that big monthly mortgage repayment, or rent bill, hanging over your head each month.

How a mortgage works

When most people go to buy a house they don't actually have the purchase price sitting in their bank account. They have just a fraction of that, and borrow the rest from the bank. That loan is known as a mortgage. The amount borrowed, plus interest, is paid back to the bank over a number of years.

Interest

You can decide whether you want to fix the interest on your home loan, go for a variable rate, or split it. Fixed interest is where the interest is set at a certain level for a particular period of time. A variable interest rate moves up and down with the official interest rate set by the Reserve Bank. A split rate is where you mix both the fixed and variable rates, to give you the best of both worlds.

Repayments

Mortgage repayments are usually made on a monthly basis. The rule of thumb is that repayments on the mortgage should not exceed 30 percent of your gross income. If they do exceed that amount, you are considered to be in "mortgage stress".

The ability to pay big lump sums or small, but regular, extra payments on your home loan is the key to paying it off quickly and reducing the overall interest charged.

Redraw Facilities

Redraw facilities allow any extra repayments you make, above the minimum monthly repayment, to be withdrawn at a later date. This allows you to funnel all your savings into the home loan now, reducing the principle amount borrowed, and redraw the money if you really need it for something else down the track.

A redraw facility essentially turns a home loan account into a savings account as well. The big banks usually call this an offset account.

Mortgage Insurance

If you borrow more than 80 percent of the purchase price from the bank you will also have to pay mortgage insurance. This covers the banks expenses if you default on the loan and they then have to sell the property to get their money back.

Your options

If you chose to spend your lump sum on your place of residence, there are a few ways you can do it.

Buy out your partner

In most situations, you and your partner will each get half of the equity in your home following the property settlement. If you are keen to stay in your current house, you may chose to use your lump sum to buy your partner's stake in your family home. If you don't buy your partner out, they are likely to want to sell the house so they can get to their cash.

Pay off part of the current mortgage

If your partner chooses to keep their stake in the house as an investment, you could use your lump sum to pay off a chunk of the mortgage. This will reduce the amount your end up paying in interest and could take years off the life of the mortgage.

Downsize

What many friends have done is sell the family home, their partner gets their stake, and then they buy something a bit smaller and cheaper with their share.

Once they put their stake in the old house and their lump sum together, they can often buy a smaller house outright. This then reduces ongoing financial pressures, because there are no mortgage repayments to make.

Remember – your lump sum from the property settlement is all you are going to get from your former partner, aside from payments to cover day-to-day expenses of children under 18. The lump sum is meant to account for any loss of earning capacity, if you spent time at home looking after your children, and your share of superannuation and investments. If you invest the entire lump sum in your place of residence, you will need to seek some other form of income to build up future superannuation and investments.

> Remember Sarah from step 3. She and her husband split their property 50-50. While she would have been able to buy her husband out of the family home, she didn't feel very attached to the place and chose to sell it.
>
> Sarah bought a smaller, less expensive, house for herself and her two children and ended up with a little bit left over to invest. Now she has no rent or mortgage payments to make, and can afford to save and invest a chunk of her current income.

INVESTING IN THE STOCK MARKET

Shares have historically outperformed other assets like property and bank deposits over the long term, and it's unlikely to be any different in the future.

Investing your lump sum in the stock market gives you the chance to make big gains, but it also exposes you to big losses. Before you leap into any kind of investment, you need to do your homework.

Don't jump in and out of shares as markets fluctuate on a daily basis. The best way to steadily build your wealth is to use informed investment advice and buy stocks for the long-term.

A lesson on the stock market

Buying shares is like buying part of a company. You become one of the owners, along with thousands of other people. Telstra, for example, has over one and a half million individual shareholders.

> **Investing your lump sum in the stock market gives you the chance to make big gains, but it also exposes you to big losses.**

You make money from the share market, which is also know as the equity market, when shares go up in price or when they pay a dividend. A dividend is your share of the company's profits.

Shares are traded on the stock exchange, which is like a big electronic market. People come to the stock market to buy and sell shares through stockbrokers, who are like the stall owners at a market.

If there are more people wanting to buy a share in a company, compared to the number who want to sell, then the price goes up.

With a bank account you never lose the money you put in, but shares are different. Shares can go down, as well as up in value, and there may be periods

Investing Your Share | STEP 5

where the value of your shares is actually less than what you paid for them. Sometimes companies can go broke, like HIH and OneTel, and you lose everything you invested.

Share investing is riskier than putting money into the bank, but there is the potential to make a lot more money when times are good. The key is to buy shares in good solid companies.

When investing in shares you will hear a lot about the All Ordinaries Index. This is like a barometer of stock market health. It measures the price movement of shares in 500 companies. So if the All Ordinaries Index is going up, then most share prices are going up as well, and that's a good thing. When the All Ords is going down, then most share prices are going down, and that's bad for shareholders. The S&P ASX200, is similar to the All Ords, except it measures the price movements of the 200 biggest companies on the Australian Stock Exchange.

Every year listed companies are required to produce an annual report. It is like a report card on the company, which shows what the company has been doing and how it has performed. If you hold shares in a company you can request a hard copy of the annual report to be sent to you, or you can view it online on the company's website.

The problem with annual reports is, unless you're an accountant, they can be very tricky to read. But don't just toss it aside, as tempting as that may be, try and at least read through at the summaries at the start of the report. The annual report may help you make decisions regarding your investment in the company.

Companies invite their shareholders to come along to annual general meetings. You are given an update on the business, get to quiz company directors and are often asked to vote on some company business. Company directors are there to represent all shareholders and keep the company's management in line. Don't be intimidated by AGMs, ask as many questions as you like. Remember, if you hold shares in a company you are effectively one of its owners.

There are lots of thinks you can do to educate yourself on the stockmarket.

- ❑ Read the weekly personal finance sections in the daily newspapers and try and tackle the daily business section of the newspaper.

- ❑ Grab some personal investment magazines. Try the Australian Financial Review's Smart Investor or Money magazine.

- ❑ Do a course. Ring the stock exchange in your capital city and find out what courses they have on offer. The ASX runs everything from free online courses to lunchtime or evening seminars run by an expert.

Your options

Stockbroker

For a fee, a stockbroker buys and sells shares on your behalf. They also do a lot of research on different companies that offer shares. For example, they rate the performance of a company, try and predict how profitable the company will be in the future, and where they see its share price going.

A stockbroker will put a portfolio of shares together for you. This portfolio should be spread over a range of sectors, so if one goes through a slump you can still make money from other areas. This portfolio should also consider your investment goals. For example, if you are after solid long-term gains your portfolio should focus on low-risk investments.

When looking for a stockbroker, start by asking your family and friends who they use. Your financial planner should also be able to help you in this area.

Online trading

Online trading is where you buy and sell shares yourself over the internet. You can do this by becoming a member of sites like www.etrade.com.au and www.commsec.com.au.

This is a much cheaper than using a stockbroker. Each time you make a trade online you have to pay some kind of fee, usually around $30. The downside is you have to do all the research yourself and make the big decisions. However, the site you join should provide you with some kind of basic research on companies.

Online trading is not for first time investors, unless you have someone experienced guiding you.

Managed fund

If you want to invest in shares, but are a bit nervous about taking the plunge, doing it through a managed fund is a good alternative.

A managed fund is where a whole bunch of people pool their savings. Expert fund managers then decide where to invest that money, and buy and sell on everyone's behalf. Because a bunch of other people are putting their money with yours, there is much more to invest and the fund can buy shares in a number of companies. That means all your eggs are not in the one basket, and if one share is a dud the others will hopefully be doing a lot better.

Managed funds are also a great way to pick up tips on how professionals invest in the stock market. Your fund manager will send your regular statements and newsletters explaining what they are doing and why.

The longer you are prepared to invest, the more attractive a growth fund becomes. Here the manager invests looking for higher gains, which are likely to come with higher risks. However, if you're investing for at least five years, history shows you'll do pretty well out of a growth portfolio.

A balanced fund looks for more stable returns and spreads money more evenly over different assets. Say 70 percent in shares, 20 percent in fixed interest, and 10 percent in property. The risks aren't as high, but neither are the returns.

Most of the big financial companies offer managed funds; the likes of Macquarie Bank, BT, AMP, and Colonial First State to name a few. If you go to their websites you can view prospectuses online. Each prospectus will explain what kind of stocks a particular fund invests in, how it's performed over the last few years, and what the entry costs are to the fund.

The financial planner

Your financial planner will help you form a personal investment strategy based on your goals, risk appetite and financial resources.

According to the Financial Planning Association, financial planners use a six-step process to help you take a 'big picture' look at where you are and where you want to be financially.

1) They get all your financial data together. Thinks like details on your income, debt level and financial commitments.

2) They get you to identifying your goals. For example, when you would like to retire and what kind of lifestyle you would like to lead.

3) They then identify any financial issues, or deficiencies, between where you are now financially and where you want to be.

4) The next step is preparing your financial plan. In this they will recommend what investments they think you should get into, and the associated risks.

5) They then implement your financial plan, and put you into the investments you have selected.

6) They will continually review and revise your plan to make sure it's current, and relevant to changing market conditions and your lifestyle.

Fees

The services of a financial planner don't come cheap, but just think of the money they will hopefully help you earn. You need to go and shop around for a financial planner until you find the person who is going to work best for you. Make sure you fully understand their fees and how they work, and the financial planner understands your goals.

You will often pay a one-off fee for getting advice. A basic financial plan is likely to cost you around $1,000, while a more complex financial plan may be closer to $4,000. The Financial Planning Association says costs rise with the level of services provided. The fees charged depend on how complex your situation is, the qualification of the advisor, the frequency of review and the level of support you require.

After a financial planner has devised a plan for you, they can then implement your plan and mange your money…for a fee of course. The Financial Planning Association says in addition to the initial advice fee, other costs may include:

- ❑ An implementation cost. This is often a percentage of the amount you are investing.

- ❑ An ongoing advice fee. This may be in the form of commissions or bonuses on financial products you invest in.

Keep in mind some financial institutions may pay your financial planner bigger commissions than others. You want to make sure your financial planner is recommending a particular investment because it is best for you, not because it pays them the biggest kickback.

> You need to go and shop around for a financial planner until you find the person who is going to work best for you.

Make sure you fully understand your financial planner's fee structure and estimate how much you are likely to be charged. Often people don't understand how much it will actually cost until they are sent the bill. For example, if your financial planner says they charge a 2.5 percent implementation cost, work that out in dollar terms. If you are investing $500,000 that's an annual fee of $12,500. It doesn't seem a lot of money in percentage terms, but it may when you do your sums.

> Once the financial settlement was resolved Sarah realised she quickly had to learn how to take care of her finances herself – and she was petrified. Sarah describes that period as a 'nightmare'. Friends rallied round and pointed her in the right direction.
>
> A financial advisor was suggested and, though the thought terrified her, Sarah started on the road to complete financial independence. Sarah had meetings with her advisor and established a financial plan for her future.
>
> She is now much more confident with the process and is pleased she didn't put it off, as she would rather have done. She now feels more in control, but not alone in her decision-making. Sarah doesn't have a problem handling her day-to-day finances and working to a budget to meet her family's needs.

Stock market dos and don'ts

Rule 1 Do your homework before buying. Don't buy or sell on rumour, hunch or impulse. Get hold of broker reports and the company's last annual report, read the financial press and, of course, talk to friends and relatives who already invest in shares or work for a stockbroker, financial planner or accountant.

Rule 2 Balance the risk with the rewards. If what you read and hear suggests the share has more chance of falling in price than rising, don't buy. Look closely at past performance and future prospects. Remember the sleep test. If the worry of your shares falling keeps you awake at night, don't buy them.

Rule 3 Keep checking after you've bought. Investment conditions can change, company management can change, a company's objectives can change. Review your shares at least once every six months to see how they're going.

Rule 4 Be patient and don't expect to become wealthy overnight. Most shares will need at least a year to show some reasonable appreciation.

Rule 5 Don't forget you can earn an income from shares and cash management trusts. A share is a part ownership in a company; you receive dividends when the company makes a profit. With a cash management trust, you are lending the trust your money which they pay you interest on, so your income goes up when the unit price rises.

Rule 6 Be prepared for unexpected events. If the event concerns any of your shares, don't panic. Review the situation promptly before taking any action. For instance, a sudden drop in a share price may well mean a big investor has sold a large parcel of shares, and more often than not the prices rebounds within a day or two.

Women's Guide To Going it Alone

Rule 7 Don't try to back every horse in the race. It's far better to hold a smaller number of shares, which you know well and are comfortable with, than to invest in a lot of companies in the hope of picking more winners.

Rule 8 Take a loss quickly. Don't let pride or stubbornness prevent you from accepting a mistake and correcting it. One big profit makes up for a lot of little losses.

Rule 9 Follow the market, don't try to beat the trend. In bear markets (when stocks are down) be cautious, in a fluctuating market think twice, and in bull markets (when prices are booming) take greater risks.

Rule 10 It's better to make a little less profit by selling too soon, than to take the risk and hold onto a stock in the hope good times will keep going and then they don't.

INVESTING IN PROPERTY

Property is generally considered to be a safe investment compared to the stock market. It's a physical asset you can check up on. But, like the markets, property goes through troughs and peaks. To secure good returns you need to understand the process and do your homework.

The main advantages of investing in property are capital growth and the tax advantages of negative gearing.

Buying an investment property

An investment property doesn't have to be something you can see yourself living in. A small apartment on a busy street in the city can still deliver good returns.

Returns

When choosing an investment property you need to look at how much the value of your property is likely to appreciate. That's the capital growth. Groups like Australian Property Monitors provide information on recent sales and forecast returns for particular areas.

During boom times, property prices may double in value in the space of a few years. But there are also years when you will get almost no growth. Historically, property grows steadily.

Pick a region

When picking a region to invest in you have to be smart. Don't choose a location where you would like to live, choose one that will generate the best returns.

Women's Guide To Going it Alone

Buy in a growth area. The general rule is suburbs within 10 kilometres of the city centre will offer the best growth. You also need to look for things like proximity to transport, shops and facilities like parks and ovals. All these factors will increase the amount of rent you will be able to get and support the sale price when you move on.

Select a property

Again, you can't just go for what you would want. You need to choose a property based on how easy it would be to rent out or sell if you needed to get rid of it in a hurry.

> **Set a limit and don't go above that. If you miss out on one property, something else will come on the market.**

In general, units are easier to rent out than houses. People who are at the stage of life where they want to live in a unit often don't want the commitment of a mortgage, want to live closer to the city, and don't have children. While people who are after a house are generally ready to settle down and like the security of owning their own home.

Units are also easier and cheaper to maintain. You don't have to mow the lawn, weed the garden or paint the fence. If something major happens to the building, the cost of repairs is split between all the units.

Extra features that can allow you to charge more rent are a balcony, garage and internal laundry.

Getting finance

Shopping around for a home loan has never been more important. Banks see investment properties as being riskier than owner occupied properties and, as a result, may charge a higher interest rate.

When buying an investment property, don't cut any corners. Research property prices in the area and make sure you're paying fare value, conduct inspections, and most importantly do your sums. Find out how much your mortgage repayments will be each month and how much rent you can expect to get. Can you afford to make up the difference?

Don't forget to budget for stamp duty and the ongoing strata fees (generally payable quarterly), council fees and water rates. If you plan to lease your property through a real estate agent, take into account their fee, which could be anywhere from 5 to 10 percent of your weekly rental income.

Real estate agents

The golden rule when dealing with real estate agents is don't be intimidated, you are making one of the biggest purchases you are ever going to make. Don't feel pressured to make an offer on a property, wait until you're absolutely sure.

If you feel negotiating with a real estate agent is too intimidating, you can get someone else who's experienced in buying or selling property to do it for you. Maybe a parent, sibling or close friend.

Remember the price the seller asks is generally higher than what they expect to get, so start the bidding low and don't appear too keen. Put in a low offer, at least 5 percent below what they're asking, to sound them out. Then come up gradually until you can agree on a price. It's all about playing your cards right.

Set a limit and don't go above that. If you miss out on one property, something else will come on the market. Remember, it's an investment property not your home, so don't get emotionally attached.

Tax advantages

There are significant tax advantages if you negatively gear an investment property. Negative gearing is where you borrow to invest, and the amount of rent you get from a property over the year is less than the annual interest paid on the loan.

If you negatively gear a property, costs of owning that investment property are tax deductible. Costs include the interest you paid on your mortgage over the period, property management fees, and maintenance costs.

When it comes time to do your tax return, the negative income from your investment property can offset positive income from other areas and reduce your overall tax bill.

Remember not to overcommit yourself just to get a large tax deduction, which doesn't arrive until the end of the financial year. You will still have to make the mortgage repayments each month.

After you have had the investment property for a while you may stop incurring losses. Once you become positive geared, and your rental income exceeds your mortgage repayments, your tax situation will change. You will no longer have the tax deductions associated with negative gearing. Don't rush out of the investment without getting some tax advice. While you have to pay more tax, you are making money on the property.

Capital gains tax (CGT) is charged on any capital gains you make on the sale of an asset. You have to pay CGT if your capital gains are great than your capital losses in a financial year. You don't pay CGT on your place of residence, but you do on investment properties.

Investing Your Share | **STEP 5**

PUT IT INTO SUPER

You need to make sure that when you reach retirement age you will have enough superannuation to maintain your lifestyle.

If you and your partner split the super in your settlement, you will also need to start a new super account. This account could be in the fund where the original one was, or somewhere else. It depends on what you want and what the fund allows.

When you receive your share of the super, you can't just go and spend it. It has to be kept in a superannuation fund until you reach retirement age.

If you split it so your partner gets the super and you get the house, you need to establish your own super fund to provide for your retirement.

Currently, most of the retirees who rely just on the government's Age Pension are women. Once your divorce has been finalised, you need to start planning for your own retirement. Superannuation will supplement the Age Pension and give you greater financial independence and security in retirement. It also helps you learn more about the investment market.

Tax advantages

Not only is putting more of your property settlement into super a good investment, but it's also tax effective.

The returns you earn in your super fund are taxed at a maximum rate of 15 percent. If you had that money invested outside of superannuation it would be taxed at the marginal rate, which could be as high as 45 percent.

If you are self-employed or not working you can claim a big tax deduction on super contributions. For example, you can receive a deduction of up to $100,000 a year if you are over 50 years old.

If you are only in your 30s, retirement may seem a long way off, and you may not be interested in building your super. That would be a mistake. You should take advantage of interest on your savings compounding in this low tax environment.

Establishing your own super fund

Superannuation is money that is put aside for retirement. Money is paid into a super fund, which is an investment scheme that accepts super contributions and invests them so their value increases before they are paid to you when you retire.

If you earn over $450 (before tax) a month, your boss has to pay 9 percent of your earnings into a super fund. Usually you can choose the super fund you want your contributions paid into.

What to look for in a fund

Five questions to ask yourself before signing your super away to a fund are:

- ❏ Who is administering the fund?
- ❏ Who is managing (investing) the fund?
- ❏ Where are the assets invested?
- ❏ What are the administration costs?
- ❏ What are the penalties, if any, for stopping contributions or withdrawing?

Before you commit to a fund you need to consider your risk profile. Do you want to invest in a high-risk fund, which has the potential to deliver substantial returns and losses? Or would you prefer a low-risk fund, which is unlikely to deliver high returns or losses? Or something in between? Most people go for a balanced fund. You also have the option of choosing whether you want to invest in Australian stocks, overseas markets, or different sectors like property. You don't want to be too cautious, or else you'll end up with a smaller super payout. On the other hand, you shouldn't take on so much risk that you could blow the lot.

Make sure you go with a reputable fund manager with a good track record. The government doesn't guarantee the safety of super, so it's up to you to find out how the money is invested and be happy it's invested safely. Choose a fund manager that provides you with regular detailed updates of where your money is being invested and how it's performing.

Many super funds offer extra features like insurance cover for death and disability at cheaper rates and low interest home loans.

Super contributions

If you have, or get, a job your employer will take 9 percent out of your salary and put it into your super fund.

You can also choose to contribute extra money into your fund. This will then get taxed at just 15 percent, instead of your regular marginal tax rate which could be higher. The government also adds extra incentives. For example, if you earn less than $58,980 a year the government will contribute up to $1.50 for every $1 you voluntarily contribute up to a maximum co-contribution of $1,500 a year.

Self managed super funds

You can also choose to contribute your super to an independently managed super fund or to a self-managed super fund.

There are over 300,000 self-managed super funds in Australia. Like regular funds, a self-managed super fund invests contributions that you can access when you retire. The difference is the members of these fund are also the trustees. It is the trustees who determine where their contributions are invested, and they can't receive any remuneration for their services. Self-managed super funds have to have four or fewer members.

A self-managed super fund doesn't have the fees of a regular fund, because you manage it yourself. On the other hand, it doesn't have experienced fund managers selecting where to invest your contributions. This alternative is only for people who have experience in investing or are under the guidance of someone who does, like a parent or sibling.

You are also limited in what you can invest in. It's harder to get into things like overseas shares, sought-after initial public offerings, and sophisticated investments that only the big fund managers have access to. Today self-managed super funds have the biggest chunk of their assets invested in local listed shares. Only a small number invest in international shares.

BUY A BUSINESS

If you have a lump sum to invest and plan to look for a new job, why not combine the two and establish or buy a business?

This might be a scary thought for some people, but if you think you have a unique idea or spot something you think you could develop, why not give it a go?

Buying or setting up a business can be very rewarding, but it is not something that you should treat lightly.

Can provide good returns

Owning your own business gives you the potential to earn much more than you would in a regular job, and possibly greater returns than an investment property or a share portfolio. The problem is the risk. Your business may also struggle to turn a profit, and not just in the short-term.

If you find a potential business or think of a good idea, do the sums with your accountant before you leap into this kind of investment. How many products or hours of service would you have to sell each month to be profitable? How much would the initial investment in the business be? Would you need help from the bank?

If you do decide to run your own business, don't put all your eggs in one basket. Maybe invest part of your lump sum in the business, and put the rest in a safer investment.

Something to do

Being self-employed means you are your own boss. You are responsible for your success or failure.

The major benefit of being self-employed is you have the potential to earn more if you are successful, although you will often have to work longer and harder hours when you work for yourself. Other benefits include working when you want to and hopefully doing what you like to do best.

The downside is long working hours, the stress of whether the business will survive, and not receiving a regular income. But for many people, the possible success outweighs the risk of failure.

Buy into an area that is a hobby

If you have a particular hobby that you are passionate about, why not try and develop a business around it. What better job is there than doing what you love!

If you love cooking, have you thought about a catering business? If you are an avid kayaker, what about running tours or lessons in your area?

If you do decide to set up a business in an area you love, you still have to put in the same amount of research, time and effort if you want to make it work.

What to consider

Do you buy an existing business or start one up

If you opt to set up a business from scratch you need to come up with an idea for a business, which is often the biggest challenge. This idea should take advantage of your skills, experience and, most importantly, what you know best.

Decide what you are good at and what you like doing. A great way to do this is to draw up three lists;

List 1	List 2	List 3
What I'm good at	Skills	What I like doing
This is fairly easy, as you list your natural talents and strengths of your personality.	Think about what qualifications you have and what you have learned from jobs you've had before.	When you write this list make sure you don't limit yourself, as businesses can relate to just about any interest possible.

Investing Your Share | **STEP 5**

Study the lists and see if they guide you toward a business idea that would suit you.

When trying to come up with an idea, take a look at what the market needs. Research the industry you want to go into, your market and your competition.

Success rates

Being your own boss isn't all fun and games. There are some very sobering statistics around showing just how many small businesses go broke compared to how many are successful. The importance of properly researching your business options can't be stressed enough.

To increase your chances of success, make sure you complete this checklist:

- ❑ Get advice from people who have had experience in this area before you start.

- ❑ Research and determine your market.

- ❑ Write a business plan setting out what you want to achieve and how you plan to achieve it.

- ❑ Don't pursue the idea if you have the slightest doubts; you need to be 100% committed.

- ❑ Would you employ you to do the job?

ESTATE PLANNING

Nothing is forever and funeral columns remind us of that every day. It is really important you plan for the worst and update your will every time your circumstances change, for example separating from your partner.

Why it's important to put together a will

A will is a legal document that states how you would like your assets to be distributed after your death. Around 40 percent of Australians don't have a will. If you die without a will, the government may decide how to divide your estate. The last thing you want is your money, property and belongings going to the wrong people.

You need to make a new will each time a major shift in your personal life occurs; marriage, divorce or entering a de facto relationship.

After your separation or divorce speak to a lawyer about the status of your will. Has your divorce made your existing will invalid? Has it cancelled any payout or distribution of gifts to your ex-partner? Are they now barred from carrying out roles such as executor of your will or trustee of your estate?

You can make a new will that cancels an earlier will. It can either state all earlier wills are cancelled or the terms of the new will can contradict those of an earlier will.

Is your ex-partner still the beneficiary of your superannuation? If so, also remember to change that when you are updating your will.

How to do a will

A will is not valid unless it is in writing (typed or handwritten), signed and witnessed.

These days formal requirements have been relaxed and the Courts are more willing to accept a document as a will if it is satisfied it is what the deceased person wanted.

In your will you need to state exactly who you want what assets to go to. For a will to be valid it has to meet certain criteria:

- ❑ You must be over 18 years old.

- ❑ It must be in writing, whether it be handwritten, typed or printed.

- ❑ You must sign it.

- ❑ It must be signed by at least two witnesses who are not beneficiaries or a spouse of a beneficiary.

- ❑ You must know the legal effect of your will, be aware of the extent of your assets, and the people who are expected to benefit from your estate.

(The Public Trustee of New South Wales)

There is no excuse for you not to have an up-to-date will. If your will is very simple, you can write one yourself. The Post Office and newsagencies have will kits to help you do this. These wills must still be signed and witnessed properly.

If your will is a bit more complex, it is best to use a lawyer.

Once you have put together a will make sure it doesn't contradict anything else. For example, make sure the superannuation beneficiary you have nominated to your super fund is the same beneficiary you have nominated in your will.

STEP 6

DIVIDING RESPONSIBILITIES

Women's Guide To Going it Alone

If you and your ex-partner have children together you can't finalise the property settlement and maintenance arrangements and then burn your bridges. You will have a relationship with this person for the rest of your life. Think of all the special birthdays, graduations, sporting grand finals, and dance recitals…let alone the big things with all the family, like 18ths, 21sts and weddings.

You and your ex-partner both need to play a role in your children's lives and manage a long-term relationship, no matter how strained it is.

COUNSELLING

Counselling for your children should not stop after the initial separation period. It should continue for as long as it is necessary. You don't want your children holding on to any issues that will affect them emotionally later down the track.

Professional

Your kids shouldn't be expected to adapt to their new living situation on their own. A counsellor has experience helping children understand what is happening and why. They also know what signs to look for to make sure the message is getting through to your kids.

Make sure you also inform the school counsellor about the permanent changes to their living situation. They can then look out for any behavioural problems at school.

At home

There are a number of things you can do to help your children during this time of transition. Family Court Counsellors and members of the medical profession have looked at the effects of divorce on kids. They have put together a number of guidelines, which are a good place to start:

- Repeated simple explanations and answering all their questions can help children adjust to their new living situation. Under no circumstances should you keep your kids in the dark.

- Give your kids time to adjust to their new way of life. Give them time to adjust to dad not reading them a story every night, and to only having the attention of one parent at a time not two.

- Try and be more available to your children than you have been in the past.

- Reassure your kids that they are not to blame for your marriage break-up. That they haven't done anything to make the other parent go away.

- Don't let the divorce affect the way you discipline your kids. They need consistency.

- Encourage your children to talk about their feelings. According to Relationships Australia even small worries, like whether or not they can still afford to go to dancing classes or tennis lessons, can build up in a child's mind.

- If you happen to cry in front of your kids, made sure you tell them why. Don't let them try and figure it out for themselves. They may feel guilty for you being upset, and think it's because of something they have done.

- When talking to them about the break up of your marriage, try to emphasise the positive aspects. Tell your kids about the good times. This should help them realise they don't have to take sides.

- Encourage your ex-partner to introduce your kids to their new living conditions. They shouldn't try and hide them. A lot of parents make the mistake of not showing their kids where they live, and deliberately organising activities out and about…like restaurants, the movies and the zoo.

❑ When your children visit your ex-partner listen with interest about what they did. Don't treat it like the Spanish Inquisition and fire questions at them.

CO-PARENTING

You and your ex-partner need to put aside any feelings of resentment and anger when you make decisions about your children. You need to be cooperative parents for your children's sake.

Just because you want to have limited contact with your ex-partner doesn't mean your children should have to. You need to make a conscious effort not to put up barriers between your kids and their father. Don't bad mouth him in front of them, don't get them to spy on him for you and don't treat your kids like postmen…delivering hostile messages on your behalf. Get professional help if you need support in carrying out what is right for your kids.

> **Your kids shouldn't be expected to adapt to their new living situation on their own.**

Counsellors can really help you manage the changed situation. You could attend sessions with your ex-partner, and get counsellors to help you work out how you can responsibly parent your children in the changed situation.

Relationships Australia offers education and parenting courses to help you with the transition process. It has some great advice on how you should handle your new co-parenting responsibilities.

According to Relationships Australia, you and your ex-partner have to respect each other's privacy. Do not interfere in each other's households.

You and your ex-partner should extend common courtesy and manners when you meet, just like you would with a colleague or an acquaintance. Make appointments to discuss things. Relationships Australia suggests meeting on neutral ground, like in a coffee shop, as it can be easier to stay calm in a public place. Be business like and keep your feelings in check. When you agree on something you should put it in writing, that way everything is crystal clear. Make sure agreements and plans detail things like time, place and cost.

If something is really bothering you, you shouldn't hold your anger in. Remember, your children will benefit from a good resolution to your differences. When you are sorting out a heated issue make sure you don't do it in front of your children. The last thing they want to see is you fighting, they are trying to get used to their new situation.

Don't just pick faults in your ex-partner, or the situation, actively look for solutions. No matter how angry you are, don't deliberately try to hurt your partner. Don't do thinks like threaten to take the kids away or limit their access. If you can't reach a solution, you could always get someone else to mediate.

Once you have reached a solution to a particular issue, tell your kids about it. According to Relationships Australia, children need to know how you have decided to settle the difference.

You need to follow through on set agreements you make. Once arrangements for the children are in place, stick to them. Your kids need certainty, not constant changes.

If you hear that your ex-partner broke his side of the bargain through your kids, give him the benefit of the doubt before you go off your rocker. Go straight to him and calmly check out the facts.

With so many changes taking place for your children try and nurture your own relationship with them, in your own way. Let your ex-partner do the same.

Dividing Responsibilities | **STEP 6**

TIME WITH THE KIDS

You and your ex-partner may have agreed on a set routine for your children, but what about all the extras occasions that come up? Do you still stick to the common 'weekdays and one weekend at mum's and every second weekend at dad's'?

Set visits

If you have your children full-time, make sure you give them lots of notice about visits with their dad. Chat to them about it and encourage them to look forward to it and get excited.

If your ex-partner has your children full-time, make sure you plan your access visits well in advance. It is really important to arrive on time. According to experts, children see lateness as a lack of interest or love. It's good to call your kids on the day of the visit, to reassure them you will be there on time and that you are really looking forward to it. That will help them relax in the hours before you arrive.

You and you ex-partner need to agree on exactly where the kids will be picked up from and dropped off and at what time. When you do the exchange, don't leave your kids stranded on a footpath. Go up to the door with them and see them over to the other parent. The more reassured your children are, the easier this process will be on them.

Extras

Once you have set up a regular routine of who looks after the children when, you need to discuss what happens when other things pop up.

If each parent has the children every other weekend, does this mean they are only allowed to go watch them play sport, for example, on the weekend they are with the kids? Or are both parents able to turn up every week?

What about special events that fall outside the set visits timetable? What if a grandparent on your ex-partner's side is in town visiting? Are you going to be flexible and swap weekends or is there no grey area?

What happens when your children get sick? Should the parent that has the kids full-time be the one to take the day off work to look after them, or do both parents share this duty?

These are just some of the things you need to think about and discuss with your ex-partner. Remember to keep your children's best interests at heart; don't be vindictive.

Not matter what you decide about your level of flexibility on the issues above, there are many things both you and your ex-partner will have to attend no matter who has the kids. It is important to your children that both parents turn up for special things like school plays and dance recitals, important presentations, and parents' days at school.

Holidays

You can't forget to plan ahead for the holidays. There will be some very tough decisions here, which will require calm discussion.

You need to work out who will look after the children on special occasions like Christmas and birthdays. Decide on this well in advance and let your children know what's going on. You can't treat these as regular days in the visits cycle. Your kids will more than likely want to see both their parents.

Many of the divorced families we know will organise for their kids to have Christmas lunch with one parent and dinner with the other. They then swap this each year, so they get a turn of having the children on Christmas morning. Birthdays are a bit more complicated, because five times out of seven everyone has to go to work and school. If you and your ex-partner are on good terms with each other, why not have a combined birthday dinner celebration? If you're not, the child could celebrate with one parent on their actual birthday, and the other parent the next day or on the weekend.

School holidays are another area you need to discuss. Does the parent who has the children full-time have to cover all the school holiday arrangements?

What about vacations? Do you try and get into a routine here, where you each get to take the kids away someplace every other school holidays, or will you be flexible and make decisions about vacations as they come?

ADULT CHILDREN

Adult children are a different ball game altogether. It is up to them which parents they see, how regularly, and where they live. Don't underestimate the effect your divorce will have on adult children. Although they will fully understand what's happening, your decision to divorce can be just as upsetting as it is for younger children.

By the time a child is 18 or so they have generally developed a strong friendship with their parents. If one parent sparks the break-up, adult children often feel betrayed by that person.

Living arrangements

Because adult children are much more aware of what's going on, they can easily identify which parent initiated the divorce. If they feel it was for the wrong reasons, they will generally take the other person's side and live with them. An adult child can then only be encouraged to go and visit the other parent, not forced.

Alternatively, an adult child may be so upset by their parents' decision to divorce that they move out of home altogether. They would rather foot all the bills, than have to get used to a new living arrangement that's foreign to what they have grown up with all their life.

> Remember Jane from earlier in the book? Her daughter Emily was 19 when her father moved out. At the time she was still living at home with her parents and her younger brother.
>
> Emily had seen the relationship between her parents disintegrate over the years, as her father increasingly isolated himself from the family.
>
> When her father moved out of the family home there was no question about who Emily was going to live with. She was there for her mother every step of the way. Emily supported her when dealings with her father got stressful, and she spent time with her mother who would have otherwise been alone.
>
> Because Emily was so involved in the divorce process, her resentment for her father grew to the point where she has cut off most contact.

GUIDELINES

Just because a child is 18 doesn't mean they don't need your guidance and support. Besides, some 18 year olds are still at school!

You and your ex-partner need to sit down and work out how you are going to parent an adult child. You could develop a set of rules for them to abide by in your houses. I don't mean things like being in bed by 10pm and doing the dishes every night. I mean things like asking them to pay board unless they are in full-time study, only allowing friends to stay over on weekends, and only borrowing your car if they ask first.

STEP 7

MAKING SURE IT DOESN'T HAPPEN AGAIN

Women's Guide **To Going it Alone**

Making Sure It Doesn't Happen Again | **STEP 7**

Once you have finalised the divorce and the property settlement, and have helped your children adjust to their changed situation, you need to move on with your life. This is never going to be as easy as it sounds, but remember you are not alone. While the challenges you now face may seem overwhelming, many women have had to go through them. Thankfully, there are places you can turn to for support.

MOVING ON

Don't be afraid to get help moving on with your life, especially if you feel you don't know how to do this. Relationships Australia offers guidance on how your can rebuild your life after the end of a relationship. A caring family counsellor or psychologist, who you can establish a rapport with, will also be very helpful. They will take you through the grieving process, give you tips on how to manage emotionally, and support you. This is especially important if you suffer feelings of low self-esteem, often experienced by women who are left by their husbands for younger women.

> Remember Karen? She and her husband split up after he had several affairs, but they had a very smooth divorce and he was very generous. Anyway, after the settlement was finalised Karen felt very low and had a devastating time trying to continue looking after her children. She constantly felt bad about herself and lacked confidence, unlike before the break-up. These feelings of "something must be wrong with me since my husband wanted someone else" lasted a while, despite getting lots of encouragement from friends and family. She realised that she needed to give herself time to heal. Seeking professional help taught her to stop suppressing the negative feelings and let them out. This allowed her to deal with them and then recover.

Women's Guide To Going it Alone

The support of family and friends is great, but why not also join a support group of people going through a similar situation?

You've heard us mention Relationships Australia a few times. This is a not-for-profit counselling and educational network, which is government subsidised, and offers services around Australia in 100 country and metropolitan centres. They charge fees on a sliding scale of affordability. Relationships Australia offers services ranging from counselling and one-on-one coaching sessions for building strong partnerships, to groups that lend support after a separation and educational seminars.

They can be contacted from anywhere around Australia for the cost of a local call. They also offer confidential, on-line counselling. That's great for people who live in rural or remote areas, who can't access face-to-face counselling. The contact details for Relationships Australia are in the back of the book.

Where did it go wrong?

Before you can start a successful new relationship you need to determine where you went wrong the first time around. If the union ended because of an affair, you can't just blame it on that. Think about what your marriage was like before that. It couldn't have been too crash hot.

Did your marriage breakdown because you simply fell out of love, or did you grow apart, or did your drive your partner away, or vice versa, because of particular behaviour.

For example, if your marriage fell apart because you and your partner grew apart, you need to think about how that occurred. This is what happened for a few of the divorced couples that we know. They got married at a pretty young age and had children fairly young. The wife stayed home to raise the kids because that's what most people did back then, and the husband went off to climb the corporate ladder. Fifteen years or so down the track and the husband has evolved and developed new interests over the years. Meanwhile, the wife hasn't changed. Before they knew it, they weren't working on their marriage. Instead they were watching it fall apart.

Making Sure It Doesn't Happen Again | **STEP 7**

> Jane had been brought up with a father working in the financial industry who took care of all his family's money and bills. Her mother never had to worry about doing any of them, so neither did Jane in her own marriage. This meant her husband had to handle everything. He was in the construction industry, so he didn't have the natural 'know how' Jane's dad would have had.
>
> When reflecting on her failed marriage, Jane thinks the financial stress piled on her husband led to many of their problems. Money had been a contributing factor in the arguments for a while before their break up. Because Jane never knew what was going on with the family finances, she didn't realise how tight things had been and how hard her husband was finding it to manage their escalating credit debt.

Do you need to make changes?

Once you identify where it went wrong, you need to be more aware of that in your next relationship. If you feel there were some mistakes on your part, see what you can do to learn from these.

Start by being honest with yourself. You might have been blaming your partner, but was there really fault on both sides? Are there some annoying habits you can work on or even change?

Open, positive self-talk can bring about changes for the better. There's nothing wrong with saying to yourself, "yeah, I stuffed up too and looking at that from his perspective, I can see it would be annoying". If you admit these things to yourself you can try to correct that behaviour or lessen its effects on others.

Don't 'beat yourself up' though. Sometimes women try hard to please, doing what they feel is the right thing, putting the husband's needs first, and yet he'll still leave. If this is the case, he is the one with the problem, not you!

Whether or not you need to modify your outlook or actions, you do need help in coming to terms with maybe never knowing what went wrong for sure. If you have a lack of resolution, you might move on but inadvertently sabotage a new relationship. This is where help from a professional counsellor is invaluable.

> **You might have been blaming your partner, but was there really fault on both sides?**

ENTERING ANOTHER RELATIONSHIP

When deciding whether it's time, or whether you're brave enough, think about your motives. Is it because you're bored with not having a date, and have had too many movies and dinners with the kids and best friends? Or could it be that, despite having lots of loving family and friends at hand, you want someone to be in love with you?

One thing is for sure, you need to give yourself plenty of time after coming out of a relationship, as the toll of re-adjustment may not show for a while. You can be so busy making sure everyone else is alright that you forget about you. You are too busy looking after the family, with perhaps a new living arrangement, work commitments and extra responsibilities like financial and legal decisions. It could be that you need to grieve the loss of your relationship or marriage, or learn to forgive your former partner for leaving you or causing you to leave him. Either way, look after yourself and be prepared to go with your feelings and not suppress them.

Anne Hollonds, from Relationships Australia, says you have an opportunity to reflect and learn from the first relationship, and may be able to contribute more effectively to a new partnership.

There are a few things you can work on in regards to preparing for a new relationship. Research shows relationships last longer if you share similar interests and build a friendship first. The passion of attraction can be very powerful but, as you know, it slows down and you need a solid foundation to carry you through the next stages.

Choose someone who thinks of life and relationships the same way as you. Look for trust and respect, and don't rush this process, it's very important for you.

Diane, whose husband left her with two very young girls, thought the idea of a new relationship was frightening after being married for ten years. "You think that awkward part of your life was finished. The thought of having to go through courtship all over again seemed too hard."

Diane was lonely for adult company at home, but wasn't looking for a relationship when it found her. Life was hectic enough with a pre-schooler and a toddler, so when her girlfriend introduced her to Mike, a bachelor friend of hers, Diane had no expectations of anything more than a friendship.

Diane was worried Mike may not like her, as her confidence was very low after her husband abandoned her for a new love. She wondered if all other men would also not be interested in her. She had made a few physical changes like cutting her hair and loosing weight, something she says she has heard is quite common after a partner leaving.

After saying yes to a date, Diane wanted to back out when thinking about it further. Her girlfriend had the bright idea of double-dating with her husband and Diane and Mike. This was very successful. Having a number of people to spread the conversation took the pressure off Diane. They all said 'good night' together, which meant there was no awkward moment of the 'good night kiss'. They repeated this kind of date until Mike made a joke about whether Diane was brave enough to date him alone, which by that time she was!

The concept of starting a physical relationship was daunting for Diane, and the issue finally arose as the relationship deepened into what she knew was a lasting one. Being honest with each other about feeling nervous was comforting and Diane felt as though she was starting fresh, like it was her first experience. Diane says allowing plenty of time for this extension of their relationship was important to getting it right.

Considering the kids!

In a new relationship, there's going to be an obvious difference if you have children and your new partner doesn't. This can bring difficult times for you and much conflict with wanting to be a 'good mum' and yet act fancy-free like a single woman (if you think that is how he wants you to be). The reality is you can't be as spontaneous as you would be if you were child-free, and your children are your most precious assets and not to be considered second in any decision making.

While you may feel strongly about how right the new man in your life would be for you all, GO SLOWLY! While he needs to adjust to your children, they also need to adjust to him. Don't think that they have to love him straight away just because you might. They will probably warm to him in time, but be prepared to give them that. Also, if you don't rush your kids into it and the new relationship doesn't work out as you would have liked, your children will be spared from breaking an attachment.

As Anne Hollonds explains, parents need to understand their child's developmental stage and not expect more than they can handle. "Children need to re-establish the new relationship with both parents after a separation. You are a different parent now as a single parent and you shouldn't do anything to disrupt the bond with either parent," Ms Hollonds says.

PREPARING FOR MARRIAGE

So you have entered another relationship and guess what…you have found love a second time around and plan to head down the aisle. As unromantic as it seems, there are a number of bases to cover before taking the plunge.

Decisions, decisions

People are generally a lot more business-like about their second marriage. Not only have they seen what can happen if the union fails, but there are a lot of other factors to consider.

Living arrangements

When you decide to remarry, you need to sort out a lot of things before you tell people…espccially your children. They are likely to respond to the news with a barrage of questions, and you need to have the answers to reassure them.

Think about how the marriage will affect your current living arrangements. If you have the children full-time, will your new partner simply move into your current home, or will you all move in with him? If your partner has children from a previous marriage, where will they live? Will it be a modern day Brady Bunch with the two families having to fuse?

Making Sure It Doesn't Happen Again | STEP 7

> Diane instinctively knew not to rush into involving her daughters with Mike at first. But they came to really love him as he spent more time with them. Diane was lucky, Mike did not have kids of his own but really wanted to.
>
> Even though the girls loved Mike, they were easily upset by any change in their situation. When Diane and Mike decided to marry, the kids immediately had to ring their dad to see what he thought. Luckily he said he was very happy, then so were they!
>
> They gave their 'new dad' a nickname, which was special to them. Diane feels this had a lot to do with the children being well adjusted, having an ongoing loving relationship with their father and an equally close one with their step-father.
>
> Because Mike had a larger house, Diane and her girls moved in with him. Diane decided to rent hers out for a while. To make the move as smooth as possible for the girls, they were given the special task of selecting their new bedroom's décor, in Mike's home. Diane tried to make the day of the move as exciting as possible, and gave the kids a day off school, as they helped settle the new family in together.

Finances

After spending so much time getting your finances in order after your first marriage, you need to decide whether you are going to keep your finances independent this time around.

Do you want to open joint bank accounts? Or will you both keep your existing bank accounts, which you get paid into, and each pay for various expenses.

What about your investments? It is generally easier to keep everything in your name, rather than going to the expense and effort to put things like deeds of properties and share certificates in both names. However, you may like to rollover your super into your new husband's account.

It's important to remember that any spousal maintenance you were receiving from your first marriage will stop when you re-marry. Any child support you receive will continue regardless.

Pre-nups

There is no doubt asking your new partner to sign a prenuptial agreement is about as romantic as proposing at McDonald's. But if you had a particularly messy divorce the first time around, you are bound to see the benefits.

If you are going into a serious second relationship, you need to think about two things. One, do you want to enter into agreement to ensure you assets are protected for you and your children? Two, what sort of relationship is this and what are possible consequences?

What is a pre-nup?

A pre-nup is an agreement made before you get married, which details how assets should be divided in the case of a divorce.

In late 2000 legislation was passed in Australia that made prenuptial agreements legally binding. Before that, under the Family Law Act, a judge could override any such agreement if they felt another arrangement was more fair and equitable.

Most Binding Financial Agreements (BFAs or pre-nups) are based on the 'half to you and half to me' principal. Couples have been advised that BFAs are the best way to determine the outcome of any potential split. Financial advisors say that prenuptial agreements help to reduce disputes over the division of assets and associated legal costs.

A Binding Financial Agreement has to be prepared by a lawyer and signed by both you and your partner. A certificate of legal advice is also required to show that you both obtained independent legal advice on the matter.

At a cost of around $1,000, this agreement is much cheaper than a typical Family Court divorce hearing costing anywhere from $20,000 plus.

Relationship counsellors say the effect of prenuptial agreements is uncertain, but they have the advantage of clarifying the 'business side' of a marriage.

What to include in a pre-nup

A prenuptial agreement can cover lots of different issues. It can detail everything from how children can be accommodated if the marriage results in divorce to superannuation and retirement issues.

In your pre-nup you should record everything that you and your partner bring to the union and how it would be split in the case of divorce. If you go to the trouble to formulate an agreement like this, make sure everything is covered:

- ❏ Houses
- ❏ Investment properties
- ❏ Superannuation
- ❏ Shares
- ❏ Managed funds
- ❏ Family heirlooms
- ❏ Spousal maintenance if you get divorced

De facto

If you are not getting married, but are in a permanent relationship, you may need to protect your assets or ensure you are supported if the union fails.

If you are in a de facto relationship, you can get a co-habitation agreement. This is similar to a pre-nup or a Binding Financial Agreement. You can protect your assets if you split up, you can also detail maintenance payments.

It's a common misconception that de facto relationships have the same rights as a marriage. In many states there is no or limited maintenance if a de facto relationship disintegrates, even if one partner has given up their career to support the other partner. There is also no future needs allowance in many states.

BOTTOM LINE

By Libby Koch

Hopefully this book has helped you through the divorce process, and you are now on the way to building a new life for yourself and your loved ones.

It's really amazing how many divorced friends Dave and I have. In almost all cases, the husband has left the wife because he is unhappy in the marriage and they just can't connect anymore. In some of those cases, this has led him to look for love or companionship elsewhere and he has technically left his wife for another woman.

A divorce is one of the most emotionally traumatic things you can go through. The key is to try and keep your wits about you. Don't let your husband take you for a ride. Take the time to find out what your rights are, and then get the right advice.

Throughout the process you need to stick up for yourself. If you feel like your lawyer is stringing you along, and forcing you to go to court, stand up to him or her. Run the process like a business. If you are hiring someone, whether it be your lawyer, accountant or financial planner, and you feel they are not up to scratch…give them the flick. You don't want to risk not getting your fair share of the settlement, or making a bad investment decision when you get your hands on your money.

Many of my girlfriends are divorced, a lot recently. I have found that after a few really tough years they have mostly come out on top. Many of them go as far as describing the process as liberating. We hope it ends up being that way for you.

Women's Guide | **To Going it Alone**

Costs of Children 2008 Tables

The costs of children are indexed each year. The 2008 figures below apply to you if your child support period starts during 2008.

The source is: Australian Government Child Support Agency.

Table A - Costs of the children 2008: Children aged 12 years and under (apportioned between parents)			
Parents' combined child support income	1 child	2 children	3 or more children
$0 - $27,378	17c for each $1	24c for each $1	27c for each $1
$27,379 -$54,756	$4,654 + 15c for each $1 over $27,378	$6,571 + 23c for each $1 over $27,378	$7,392 + 26c for each $1 over $27,378
$54,757- $82,134	$8,761 + 12c for each $1 over $54,756	$12,868 + 20c for each $1 over $54,756	$14,510 + 25c for each $1 over $54,756
$82,135- $109,512	$12,046 + 10c for each $1 over $82,134	$18,344 + 18c for each $1 over $82,134	$21,355 + 24c for each $1 over $82,134
$109,513 - $136,890	$14,784 + 7c for each $1 over $109,512	$23,272 +10c for each $1 over $109,512	$27,926 + 18c for each $1 over $109,512
Over $136,890	$16,700	$26,010	$32,854

Table B - Costs of the children 2008: Children aged 13 years and over (apportioned between parents)			
Parents' combined child support income	1 child	2 children	3 or more children
$0 - $27,378	23c for each $1	29c for each $1	32c for each $1
$27,379 -$54,756	$6,297 + 22c for each $1 over $27,378	$7,940 + 28c for each $1 over $27,378	$8,761 + 31c for each $1 over $27,378
$54,757- $82,134	$12,320 + 12c for each $1 over $54,756	$15,606 + 25c for each $1 over $54,756	$17,248 + 30c for each $1 over $54,756
$82,135- $109,512	$15,605 + 10c for each $1 over $82,134	$22,451 + 20c for each $1 over $82,134	$25,461 + 29c for each $1 over $82,134
$109,513 - $136,890	$18,343 + 9c for each $1 over $109,512	$27,927 + 13c for each $1 over $109,512	$33,401 + 20c for each $1 over $109,512
Over $136,890	$20,807	$31,486	$38,877

Table C - Costs of the children 2008: Children of mixed ages (apportioned between parents)		
Parents' combined child support income	2 children	3 or more children
$0 - $27,378	26.5c for each $1	29.5c for each $1
$27,379 -$54,756	$7,255 + 25.5c for each $1 over $27,378	$8,077 + 28.5c for each $1 over $27,378
$54,757- $82,134	$14,236 + 22.5c for each $1 over $54,756	$15,880 + 27.5c for each $1 over $54,756
$82,135- $109,512	$20,396 + 19c for each $1 over $82,134	$23,409 + 26.5 for each $1 over $82,134
$109,513 - $136,890	$25,598 + 11.5c for each $1 over $109,512	$30,664 + 19c for each $1 over $109,512
Over $136,890	$28,746	$35,866

Finding an accountant

www.cpaaustralia.com.au

Finding a financial planner

www.fpa.asn.au

Finding a lawyer

Law Council of Australia - Family Law Section

Tel: (02) 6246 3788

website: www.familylawsection.org.au

Law Society of the Australian Capital Territory

Tel: (02) 6247 5700

website: www.lawsocact.asn.au

Law Society of New South Wales

Tel: (02) 9926 0333

website: www.lawsociety.com.au

Law Society Northern Territory

Tel: (08) 8981 5104

website: www.lawsocnt.asn.au

Law Society of Queensland

Tel: (07) 3842 5842

website: www.qls.com.au

Law Society of South Australia

Tel: (08) 8229 0222

website: www.lawsocietysa.asn.au

Law Society of Tasmania

Tel: (03) 6234 4133

website: www.taslawsociety.asn.au

Law Institute of Victoria

Tel: (03) 9607 9311

website: www.liv.asn.au

Law Society of WA

Tel: (08) 93227877

website: www.lawsocietywa.asn.au

Legal Aid Commission of New South Wales

02 9219 5000 LawAccess NSW: 1300 888 529

www.legalaid.nsw.gov.au

Victoria Legal Aid

03 9269 0234 Country callers toll free 1800 677 402

www.legalaid.vic.gov.au

Legal Aid Queensland

07 3238 3444 Cost of local call within Queensland 1300 65 11 88

www.legalaid.qld.gov.au

Legal Services Commission of South Australia

08 8463 3555 Telephone Advice free call 1300 366 424

www.lsc.sa.gov.au

Legal Aid Western Australia

08 9261 6222 Country callers toll free 8.30am - 4.30pm 1300 650 579

www.legalaid.wa.gov.au

Legal Aid Commission of Tasmania

03 62363800 Cost of local call within Tasmania 1300 366 611

www.legalaid.tas.gov.au

Northern Territory Legal Aid Commission

08 8999 3000 Country callers toll free 1800 019 343

www.ntlac.nt.gov.au

Legal Aid Commission of the ACT

02 6243 3471; 1300654314

www.legalaid.canberra.net.au

Counselling contacts

Centacare Australia – 02 62397700

Parenting and Relationship Line – 1300 365 859 (local call cost)

Relationships Australia – 1300 364 277 (local call cost)

www.relationships.com.au

Family Relationship Advice Line – 1800 050 321

Family Court

www.familycourt.gov.au

Child Support Agency

www.csa.gov.au

Government Support

Centrelink Family Assistance Office – 13 61 50

Youth and Student Services – 13 24 90

We would like to thank the following organisations for their help in putting together this book.

Prescott Securities

WHK Horwath

WattsMcCray Lawyers

Relationships Australia

Samantha Brown and Libby Koch would also like to thank Jane Wilkinson for her help researching legal aspects of this book.